Mastering OpenVAS: A Comprehensive Guide to Cybersecurity Vulnerability Assessment

Yaakov Hershkowitz

In an age defined by interconnectedness and technological innovation, the security of our digital landscapes stands as an imperative pillar of safeguarding information, infrastructure, and privacy. As organizations grapple with the ever-evolving threat landscape, mastering the art of vulnerability assessment becomes not only a best practice but a strategic necessity.

Welcome to "**Mastering OpenVAS: A Comprehensive Guide to Cybersecurity Vulnerability Assessment**." This book is designed as your companion on a journey into the depths of OpenVAS, an open-source powerhouse in the realm of vulnerability assessment. Whether you are a seasoned cybersecurity professional seeking to enhance your skills or a newcomer eager to delve into the world of proactive defense, this guide aims to equip you with the knowledge and tools needed to navigate and harness the full potential of OpenVAS.

Unveiling OpenVAS

Chapter 1 introduces you to the genesis of OpenVAS, tracing its evolution and establishing its pivotal role in the cybersecurity landscape. We will explore the roots of OpenVAS and discuss why it has become an indispensable asset for organizations committed to fortifying their defenses against an array of cyber threats.

Setting the Stage

In Chapter 2, we embark on the practical journey of setting up OpenVAS. From installation on various platforms to configuring the system and managing user accounts, this chapter lays the groundwork for harnessing the power of OpenVAS within your cybersecurity arsenal.

Navigating the OpenVAS Interface

Chapter 3 offers a guided tour through the OpenVAS interface, unraveling its dashboard, features, and customization options. Understanding how to navigate this interface efficiently is fundamental to harnessing the full potential of OpenVAS in identifying and mitigating vulnerabilities.

As we progress through subsequent chapters, we will delve into the intricacies of vulnerability scanning, interpreting scan reports, automating assessments, and advanced customization. Real-world case studies and practical examples will illuminate the application of OpenVAS in diverse scenarios, providing you with tangible insights and actionable strategies.

Why Master OpenVAS?

Mastering OpenVAS is not merely about learning a tool; it's about cultivating a mindset of proactive cybersecurity. The ability to identify and mitigate vulnerabilities before they can be exploited is a skill that transforms cybersecurity practitioners into true defenders of the digital realm.

So, buckle up and prepare to embark on a journey of exploration and mastery. "Mastering OpenVAS: A Comprehensive Guide to Cybersecurity Vulnerability Assessment" is your roadmap to becoming a proficient OpenVAS user, a vigilant cybersecurity professional, and a guardian of the digital frontier.

1. Introduction to OpenVAS

In the ever-expanding landscape of cybersecurity, where the digital realm continually intertwines with our daily lives, the need for robust vulnerability assessment tools has never been more critical. As we embark on this journey into the heart of cybersecurity preparedness, our first destination is the exploration of OpenVAS.

Unraveling the Origins

OpenVAS, short for Open Vulnerability Assessment System, emerges as a beacon in the realm of cybersecurity, casting its light upon the hidden vulnerabilities that can compromise the security of systems and networks. In this chapter, we delve into the genesis of OpenVAS, tracing its roots and understanding the evolution that has shaped it into a formidable force in the arsenal of cybersecurity professionals.

The Significance of OpenVAS

Why OpenVAS? Beyond being a mere tool, OpenVAS represents a philosophy—an approach to cybersecurity that embraces the proactive identification and mitigation of vulnerabilities. As we navigate through this chapter, we will unravel the significance of OpenVAS in the contemporary cybersecurity landscape. From its foundational principles to its role in fortifying digital defenses, we lay the groundwork for a comprehensive exploration.

What Awaits You

Embarking on the journey to master OpenVAS requires a solid understanding of its foundations. In the subsequent sections, we will guide you through the practical aspects of setting up OpenVAS, navigating its interface, and laying the groundwork for vulnerability assessments that go beyond routine scans.

So, fasten your seatbelt as we venture into the realm of OpenVAS. By the end of this chapter, you'll not only appreciate the roots of this powerful tool but also understand why mastering OpenVAS is a pivotal step in securing the digital frontiers of today and tomorrow.

1.1 What is OpenVAS?

OpenVAS, short for Open Vulnerability Assessment System, stands as a stalwart guardian in the ever-expanding landscape of cybersecurity. It is a comprehensive, open-source vulnerability scanning and management tool designed to identify, assess, and mitigate security vulnerabilities in networks, systems, and applications. Born from the collaboration of dedicated security professionals and the open-source community, OpenVAS has evolved into a robust solution that empowers organizations to fortify their digital defenses.

At its core, OpenVAS is an essential component of the broader field of vulnerability management—a proactive approach to cybersecurity that involves identifying, classifying, and mitigating security vulnerabilities before they can be exploited by malicious actors. In essence, OpenVAS serves as a sentinel, constantly scouring digital landscapes for potential weaknesses that could be exploited by cyber threats.

Origins and Evolution: Unveiling the Genesis of OpenVAS

To understand OpenVAS, one must trace its roots back to Nessus, its predecessor. Nessus, initially an open-source tool, became a pioneering force in vulnerability scanning. However, as Nessus transitioned to a proprietary model, the need for a community-driven, open-source alternative emerged. This need led to the birth of OpenVAS, ensuring that the spirit of collaborative cybersecurity persisted in an accessible and transparent manner.

OpenVAS embodies the ethos of the open-source community, embracing transparency, community collaboration, and adaptability. Its evolution is marked by a commitment to providing a tool that not only keeps pace with emerging threats but also empowers users with the flexibility to tailor their vulnerability assessments to unique organizational requirements.

Key Features and Functionality: The Arsenal of OpenVAS

OpenVAS boasts a diverse set of features that collectively form a powerful arsenal for cybersecurity professionals. Its capabilities can be broadly categorized into vulnerability scanning, configuration assessment, and risk assessment.

Vulnerability Scanning: At its core, OpenVAS excels in identifying vulnerabilities within target systems and networks. It conducts thorough scans, probing for weaknesses in software, configurations, and system components. Leveraging a comprehensive database of known vulnerabilities, OpenVAS compares the current state of systems with a vast repository of potential security issues.

Configuration Assessment: Beyond traditional vulnerability scanning, OpenVAS assesses the configurations of systems and network components. Misconfigurations can expose vulnerabilities, and OpenVAS is adept at identifying these subtle yet impactful issues. By scrutinizing configurations, it adds an extra layer of defense against potential threats arising from improper system setups.

Risk Assessment: OpenVAS doesn't merely flag vulnerabilities; it evaluates their potential impact and risk to the organization. By assigning severity levels to identified vulnerabilities, OpenVAS enables users to prioritize remediation efforts effectively. This risk-centric approach ensures that scarce resources are allocated to addressing the most critical security concerns.

User-Friendly Interface: Navigating the Cybersecurity Landscape

OpenVAS features a user-friendly graphical interface, ensuring accessibility for users with varying levels of technical expertise. The dashboard provides a comprehensive overview of the vulnerability landscape, displaying critical information such as scan results, risk metrics, and ongoing assessments. This interface serves as a centralized command center, allowing users to orchestrate vulnerability assessments with ease.

The interface facilitates seamless navigation through OpenVAS functionalities, offering intuitive controls for configuring scans, interpreting results, and customizing assessments. This user-centric design minimizes the learning curve, enabling security professionals to harness the full potential of OpenVAS without cumbersome intricacies.

OpenVAS Components: Building Blocks of Cybersecurity Vigilance

OpenVAS comprises multiple components, each contributing to its robust functionality. These components work in harmony to conduct vulnerability assessments, interpret results, and facilitate continuous monitoring. Key components include:

OpenVAS Scanner: This component is the workhorse of vulnerability scanning, responsible for probing target systems, conducting scans, and gathering data on potential vulnerabilities.

OpenVAS Manager: Serving as the brains of the operation, the Manager orchestrates the scanning process, manages scan configurations, and interprets scan results. It acts as a central hub for coordinating vulnerability assessments.

Greenbone Security Assistant (GSA): GSA provides the web-based interface through which users interact with OpenVAS. It translates complex scan data into accessible visualizations, simplifying the interpretation of results.

OpenVAS Command Line Interface (CLI): For users who prefer a command-line approach, the CLI offers a versatile alternative. It allows for advanced customization, scripting, and automation of OpenVAS operations.

Open Source and Community-Driven Philosophy: The Heartbeat of OpenVAS

Central to OpenVAS's identity is its status as an open-source tool, embodying the principles of collaboration, transparency, and community engagement. The open-source nature of OpenVAS ensures that its source code is freely available for examination, modification, and contribution by a global community of cybersecurity enthusiasts.

The community-driven philosophy facilitates rapid development, continuous improvement, and adaptability to emerging threats. Users, ranging from individual practitioners to large enterprises, contribute to the collective knowledge pool, sharing insights, creating plugins, and enhancing the efficacy of OpenVAS in real-world scenarios.

Scalability and Flexibility: Adapting to Diverse Environments

OpenVAS is designed with scalability in mind, accommodating the needs of organizations of varying sizes and complexities. Whether deployed in a small business environment or a large enterprise network, OpenVAS scales effectively to scan diverse landscapes.

Furthermore, OpenVAS embraces flexibility in its configurations, allowing users to tailor vulnerability assessments to suit specific requirements. Customization options, coupled with support for various operating systems, make OpenVAS a versatile tool adaptable to the diverse ecosystems of modern IT infrastructures.

Integration Capabilities: Harmonizing with Cybersecurity Ecosystems

In the ever-expanding toolkit of cybersecurity solutions, interoperability is crucial. OpenVAS is designed with integration capabilities, allowing it to harmonize with other security tools and workflows seamlessly. Integration with Security Information and Event Management (SIEM) systems, incident response workflows, and broader cybersecurity strategies enhances the collective resilience of an organization.

Regular Updates and Vulnerability Feeds: Adapting to Dynamic Threat Landscapes

Cyber threats evolve continuously, necessitating tools that can keep pace with the changing landscape. OpenVAS stays attuned to emerging vulnerabilities through regular updates and feeds. The community actively contributes to the vulnerability database, ensuring that OpenVAS remains a vigilant guardian capable of identifying the latest security issues.

Compliance and Reporting: Meeting Regulatory Standards

In the realm of cybersecurity, compliance with industry regulations and standards is paramount. OpenVAS facilitates compliance assessments by aligning with various frameworks and providing reporting functionalities. Whether adhering to GDPR, HIPAA, or other regulatory requirements, OpenVAS assists organizations in demonstrating their commitment to cybersecurity best practices.

Community Support and Documentation: A Knowledge-Sharing Ecosystem

The strength of an open-source tool lies not just in its code but in the community that rallies behind it. OpenVAS benefits from a vibrant community of users, developers, and cybersecurity professionals who actively engage in discussions, share experiences, and contribute to the tool's ongoing development.

Comprehensive documentation further enhances the user experience, providing guides, tutorials, and reference materials. This wealth of resources ensures that users, whether novices or seasoned practitioners, have access to the information needed to navigate OpenVAS effectively.

Conclusion: OpenVAS as a Pillar of Cybersecurity Resilience

In conclusion, OpenVAS emerges as a pillar of cybersecurity resilience—an open-source, community-driven tool that empowers organizations to proactively manage vulnerabilities and fortify their digital defenses. With its user-friendly interface, robust feature set, scalability, and integration capabilities, OpenVAS stands as a versatile ally in the ongoing battle against cyber threats.

As technology advances and threat landscapes evolve, OpenVAS remains agile, adapting to the dynamics of the cybersecurity ecosystem. Its commitment to transparency, collaboration, and accessibility positions OpenVAS not just as a tool but as a testament to the power of open-source cybersecurity solutions.

Whether you are a cybersecurity professional seeking an effective vulnerability assessment tool or an enthusiast eager to explore the intricacies of digital defense, OpenVAS beckons as a gateway to mastering the art of proactive cybersecurity.

May your journey with OpenVAS be enlightening, your defenses resilient, and your commitment to cybersecurity unwavering in the face of evolving threats.

1.2 The Evolution of OpenVAS

The evolution of OpenVAS is a captivating journey that traces its roots, development milestones, and the continuous refinement that has positioned it as a prominent force in the realm of cybersecurity. From its inception as a response to industry shifts to its current status as an open-source guardian, OpenVAS has undergone a remarkable transformation, influenced by technological advancements, community collaboration, and a steadfast commitment to cybersecurity excellence.

Genesis: A Response to Changing Tides

The story of OpenVAS begins with the evolution of Nessus, a pioneering vulnerability scanning tool developed by Renaud Deraison in the late 1990s. Nessus gained widespread popularity as an open-source solution for vulnerability assessment. However, in 2005, Nessus transitioned to a proprietary model, leaving a void in the open-source vulnerability scanning landscape.

The community's response to this shift was the genesis of OpenVAS. Driven by the ethos of collaboration and a commitment to keeping vulnerability assessment accessible, a group of dedicated security professionals and enthusiasts embarked on the development of OpenVAS. This pivotal moment marked the birth of a tool that would go on to play a pivotal role in cybersecurity ecosystems worldwide.

Community-Driven Development: Nurturing Open Source Vigilance

OpenVAS's journey is deeply intertwined with the spirit of open-source development. Embracing transparency and collaboration, the community rallied around the project, contributing code, sharing insights, and collectively enhancing the tool's capabilities. The open-source philosophy not only democratized access to advanced cybersecurity tools but also fostered a vibrant ecosystem where knowledge was freely shared.

Through community-driven development, OpenVAS evolved rapidly, incorporating features, refining algorithms, and adapting to emerging threats. The collaborative nature of the project transformed it from a tool to a communal effort—a testament to the power of collective intelligence in fortifying digital landscapes against evolving cyber risks.

Technical Advancements: Keeping Pace with Innovation

As the digital landscape evolved, so did the demands on cybersecurity tools. OpenVAS responded to this dynamic environment by integrating cutting-edge technologies and methodologies. The tool's scanning algorithms became more sophisticated, capable of identifying intricate vulnerabilities across diverse platforms and applications.

The evolution of OpenVAS also saw the introduction of advanced scanning techniques, including authenticated scans, which enabled a deeper examination of systems by leveraging user credentials. This technical prowess not only broadened the scope of vulnerability assessments but also elevated OpenVAS to a position of trust among cybersecurity professionals.

User Interface Enhancements: From Functionality to Usability

One notable aspect of OpenVAS's evolution is the continuous improvement of its user interface. Recognizing the importance of user experience in the effective deployment of cybersecurity tools, the OpenVAS team invested in creating an intuitive, user-friendly interface. This interface served as a gateway for both seasoned cybersecurity practitioners and newcomers, providing a centralized platform for configuring scans, interpreting results, and managing assessments.

The evolution of the user interface transformed OpenVAS from a powerful tool accessible to experts into a solution that could be harnessed by a broader audience. This shift played a crucial role in expanding OpenVAS's user base and cementing its status as a versatile, approachable cybersecurity tool.

Scalability and Integration: Adapting to Diverse Ecosystems

As organizations embraced digital transformation, the need for cybersecurity tools that could scale with evolving infrastructures became paramount. OpenVAS rose to this challenge by enhancing its scalability, allowing it to perform effective vulnerability assessments in both small business environments and large enterprise networks.

Furthermore, OpenVAS recognized the importance of integration within the broader cybersecurity landscape. The tool's compatibility with various operating systems, protocols, and industry standards facilitated seamless integration into diverse security workflows. OpenVAS became a collaborative partner in comprehensive cybersecurity strategies, harmonizing with other tools such as SIEM systems, incident response workflows, and risk management frameworks.

Regular Updates and Database Enhancements: Navigating the Threat Landscape

Cyber threats are dynamic and ever-evolving, requiring cybersecurity tools to remain vigilant and adaptive. OpenVAS responded to this reality by instituting regular updates and database enhancements. The community actively contributed to the vulnerability database, ensuring that OpenVAS remained well-informed about the latest threats and vulnerabilities.

These regular updates not only fortified OpenVAS's ability to identify emerging security issues but also showcased its commitment to providing users with a tool that aligned with the rapidly changing cybersecurity landscape. This responsiveness to the evolving threat landscape solidified OpenVAS's position as a proactive guardian against digital risks.

Internationalization and Global Impact: A Tool for All

The evolution of OpenVAS transcended geographical boundaries through a focus on internationalization. Recognizing that cybersecurity is a global concern, efforts were made to make OpenVAS accessible and adaptable to users around the world. Language support, documentation in multiple languages, and a commitment to inclusivity broadened OpenVAS's impact, fostering a global community of users and contributors.

Continuous Learning: Case Studies and Real-World Examples

A significant milestone in the evolution of OpenVAS was the incorporation of real-world case studies and examples into its framework. By showcasing practical applications of OpenVAS in diverse scenarios, users gained insights into its effectiveness, learned from success stories, and understood how to navigate the complexities of vulnerability assessments in real-world environments.

These case studies became a valuable resource for both novices and experienced cybersecurity professionals, offering a bridge between theoretical knowledge and practical application. They served as a testament to OpenVAS's adaptability and effectiveness in addressing the intricacies of cybersecurity challenges.

Future-Proofing: A Glimpse into Emerging Trends

As OpenVAS evolved, so did its gaze towards the future. The inclusion of a chapter on future trends in vulnerability assessment in its documentation reflected a commitment to anticipating and preparing for upcoming challenges. OpenVAS positioned itself not just as a tool for the present but as a strategic partner in navigating the uncertainties of tomorrow's cybersecurity landscape.

Conclusion: OpenVAS as a Cybersecurity Pillar

The evolution of OpenVAS is not merely a chronological progression; it is a narrative of resilience, adaptability, and community-driven innovation. From its humble beginnings as a response to industry shifts to its current status as a trusted, open-source guardian, OpenVAS has proven its mettle in the complex and ever-changing field of cybersecurity.

As it continues to evolve, OpenVAS remains a pillar of cybersecurity—a tool that empowers organizations, educates practitioners, and stands as a testament to the enduring power of open-source collaboration. The journey of OpenVAS is an ongoing saga, with each chapter contributing to its legacy as a tool that not only identifies vulnerabilities but also embodies the principles of transparency, community, and excellence in cybersecurity defense.

May the evolution of OpenVAS continue to inspire, adapt, and fortify the cybersecurity landscape against the challenges that lie ahead.

1.3 Significance in Modern Cybersecurity

In the dynamic and interconnected landscape of modern cybersecurity, OpenVAS stands as a significant and indispensable tool, playing a crucial role in fortifying digital defenses, identifying vulnerabilities, and contributing to the proactive management of cyber risks. Its significance extends across various dimensions, making it a cornerstone in the arsenal of cybersecurity professionals and organizations striving to protect their digital assets.

Proactive Vulnerability Management: Navigating the Threat Landscape

One of the primary contributions of OpenVAS to modern cybersecurity is its role in proactive vulnerability management. In an era where cyber threats evolve rapidly, waiting for an attack to occur before taking action is no longer a viable strategy. OpenVAS empowers organizations to identify and address vulnerabilities before they can be exploited by malicious actors.

By conducting comprehensive vulnerability assessments, OpenVAS provides a proactive approach to risk mitigation. It goes beyond reactive measures, enabling cybersecurity teams to stay ahead of emerging threats, prioritize remediation efforts, and create a robust defense posture against potential cyber attacks.

Comprehensive Vulnerability Scanning: Unveiling Hidden Weaknesses

OpenVAS's significance lies in its ability to conduct comprehensive vulnerability scanning across diverse digital environments. It goes beyond surface-level assessments, delving deep into systems, networks, and applications to unveil hidden weaknesses that could be exploited by cyber adversaries. This thorough scanning capability ensures that organizations have a holistic understanding of their security posture.

Through a vast and regularly updated vulnerability database, OpenVAS identifies vulnerabilities in software, configurations, and system components. This breadth of coverage is essential in addressing the multitude of potential entry points that attackers might exploit, making OpenVAS a vital asset in the pursuit of comprehensive cybersecurity.

Risk-Centric Approach: Prioritizing Remediation Efforts

OpenVAS adopts a risk-centric approach, assigning severity levels to identified vulnerabilities based on their potential impact. This risk assessment capability is significant in modern cybersecurity, where resources are finite, and organizations must prioritize remediation efforts effectively.

By categorizing vulnerabilities according to their severity, OpenVAS guides cybersecurity professionals in focusing on the most critical issues first. This strategic prioritization ensures that limited resources are allocated where they will have the most significant impact, enhancing the overall resilience of an organization's digital infrastructure.

User-Friendly Interface: Bridging the Gap for All Users

The significance of OpenVAS is amplified by its user-friendly interface, which bridges the gap between complex cybersecurity tools and users with varying levels of technical expertise. The intuitive dashboard, accessible controls, and visualizations provided by the Greenbone Security Assistant (GSA) empower users to navigate the tool effectively without being overwhelmed by technical intricacies.

This user-centric design is particularly crucial in modern cybersecurity environments, where diverse teams, including security analysts, IT administrators, and risk managers, collaborate to safeguard digital assets. OpenVAS's interface ensures that cybersecurity insights are accessible to a broad audience, fostering a collaborative and informed security culture.

Scalability and Adaptability: Meeting Diverse Organizational Needs

In the modern landscape, where organizations vary in size, complexity, and technological infrastructure, the scalability and adaptability of cybersecurity tools are paramount. OpenVAS meets this need by being scalable, accommodating the vulnerability assessment requirements of both small businesses and large enterprises.

Furthermore, OpenVAS's flexibility and compatibility with various operating systems and protocols enhance its adaptability to diverse organizational ecosystems. This adaptability ensures that OpenVAS can be seamlessly integrated into existing cybersecurity workflows, contributing to a harmonized and effective defense strategy.

Integration Capabilities: Collaborating within Cybersecurity Ecosystems

The significance of OpenVAS is accentuated by its integration capabilities, allowing it to collaborate seamlessly within broader cybersecurity ecosystems. Integration with Security Information and Event Management (SIEM) systems, incident response workflows, and other security tools transforms OpenVAS from a standalone tool into a cooperative force within the cybersecurity toolkit.

This collaborative approach enhances the overall effectiveness of cybersecurity strategies, enabling organizations to orchestrate a unified defense against evolving threats. OpenVAS's compatibility with industry standards and frameworks further cements its role as an integrated component in comprehensive cybersecurity initiatives.

Open Source Philosophy: Empowering the Cybersecurity Community

The open-source philosophy embedded in OpenVAS contributes to its significance by fostering community engagement, transparency, and collective problem-solving. The collaborative efforts of a global community of cybersecurity enthusiasts and professionals contribute to the continuous improvement and evolution of OpenVAS.

The significance of the open-source nature of OpenVAS lies in its democratization of advanced cybersecurity capabilities. Users, regardless of their organizational or financial constraints, can access, modify, and contribute to the tool's development. This inclusive model empowers the cybersecurity community to collectively address emerging challenges and share knowledge in the pursuit of a safer digital landscape.

Regulatory Compliance: Meeting Industry Standards

In an era where regulatory compliance is a critical aspect of cybersecurity, OpenVAS plays a significant role in helping organizations meet industry standards. Whether adhering to data protection laws, healthcare regulations, or financial industry standards, OpenVAS aids organizations in conducting compliance assessments.

By providing insights into vulnerabilities that might impact compliance, OpenVAS assists organizations in demonstrating due diligence and adherence to cybersecurity best practices. This significance is particularly crucial in sectors where regulatory scrutiny is high, and non-compliance can result in severe consequences.

Future-Proofing: Adapting to Emerging Threats

The modern cybersecurity landscape is characterized by rapid technological advancements and the emergence of new threat vectors. OpenVAS's significance extends to its commitment to future-proofing, as evidenced by its consideration of emerging trends in vulnerability assessment.

Through features like case studies and real-world examples, as well as a focus on future trends in vulnerability assessment, OpenVAS positions itself as a tool that adapts to evolving challenges. Its forward-looking approach ensures that organizations using OpenVAS are equipped to navigate the complexities of an ever-changing threat landscape.

Educational Resource: Bridging the Cybersecurity Skills Gap

Beyond its role as a cybersecurity tool, OpenVAS holds significance as an educational resource, contributing to bridging the cybersecurity skills gap. Its accessibility, accompanied by comprehensive documentation, case studies, and a community-driven support system, makes OpenVAS a valuable platform for learning about vulnerability assessment and cybersecurity best practices.

The educational significance of OpenVAS extends to its role in nurturing the next generation of cybersecurity professionals. Whether used in academic settings, cybersecurity training programs, or by self-learners, OpenVAS provides a hands-on learning experience, empowering individuals to develop practical skills in vulnerability management.

In conclusion, the significance of OpenVAS in modern cybersecurity is multi-faceted and profound. It serves as a proactive guardian, a comprehensive vulnerability scanner, and a collaborative force within cybersecurity ecosystems. Its user-friendly interface, scalability, integration capabilities, and commitment to open-source principles contribute to its enduring relevance in the face of evolving cyber threats. OpenVAS not only identifies vulnerabilities but also embodies the principles of accessibility, collaboration, and continuous improvement, making it a cornerstone in the pursuit of a secure digital future.

2. Setting Up OpenVAS

In the labyrinth of cybersecurity, the journey toward mastery begins with the foundational step of setting up the tools that will become our sentinels against digital threats. Chapter 2 brings us to the heart of OpenVAS, where we embark on the practical expedition of installation, configuration, and preparation for the transformative power that Open Vulnerability Assessment System (OpenVAS) brings to the forefront.

Choosing Your Path

Setting up OpenVAS is not a one-size-fits-all endeavor. Whether you find yourself on the Windows or Linux terrain, the first subchapter explores the intricacies of installing OpenVAS on various platforms. We unravel the step-by-step procedures, ensuring that, regardless of your operating system allegiance, you are equipped with the knowledge to set up OpenVAS with confidence.

Configuring the Foundations

With OpenVAS now residing on your system, the journey proceeds to the realm of configuration. In the second subchapter, we delve into the critical settings and configurations that tailor OpenVAS to the unique contours of your cybersecurity landscape. From network configurations to fine-tuning system parameters, this section ensures that your OpenVAS installation is not merely present but optimized for peak performance.

User Account Management

As we traverse the landscape of OpenVAS, the third subchapter introduces the pivotal aspect of user account management. Understanding how to create, manage, and assign permissions to user accounts is not merely an administrative task; it is the key to orchestrating a collaborative and secure cybersecurity environment.

By the conclusion of Chapter 2, you will have navigated the intricate path of setting up OpenVAS, ensuring that this powerful tool is not only operational but tailored to the unique demands of your cybersecurity initiatives. The journey into OpenVAS has just begun, and with each step, you draw closer to mastering the art of vulnerability assessment.

2.1 Installation on Windows

Installing OpenVAS on a Windows environment involves several steps to set up the required components for vulnerability scanning. While OpenVAS is typically more native to Unix-based systems, it is possible to run it on Windows using a virtual machine with a Linux distribution. The following guide outlines the process of installing OpenVAS on Windows using the Windows Subsystem for Linux (WSL).

Prerequisites:

Windows Subsystem for Linux (WSL): Ensure that you have WSL installed on your Windows machine. You can install WSL by following the official Microsoft documentation: Install Windows Subsystem for Linux.

Ubuntu or Debian on WSL: OpenVAS is well-supported on Ubuntu or Debian Linux distributions. Install either Ubuntu or Debian on WSL. You can do this by visiting the Microsoft Store and searching for "Ubuntu" or "Debian," then installing the respective distribution.

Installation Steps:

Step 1: Update and Upgrade:

Open the WSL terminal and update the package list and upgrade existing packages:

sudo apt update && sudo apt upgrade -y

Step 2: Install Required Dependencies:

Install the necessary dependencies for OpenVAS:

sudo apt install -y libopenvas9 openvas9 openvas9-manager openvas9-cli

Step 3: Configure OpenVAS:

Configure OpenVAS after the installation. This step includes creating a user and setting up the necessary databases. Follow the prompts during the setup:

sudo openvas-manage-db
sudo openvasmd --create-user=admin --role=Admin
sudo openvasmd --user=admin --new-password=<your_password>

Step 4: Start OpenVAS:

Start the OpenVAS services:

sudo systemctl start openvas-scanner
sudo systemctl start openvas-manager
sudo systemctl start openvas-gsa

Step 5: Enable Autostart (Optional):

To ensure OpenVAS starts automatically with your system, you can enable autostart for the services:

sudo systemctl enable openvas-scanner
sudo systemctl enable openvas-manager
sudo systemctl enable openvas-gsa

Step 6: Access OpenVAS Web Interface:

Open a web browser on your Windows machine and navigate to https://localhost:9392. Log in using the credentials you created during the configuration step.

Step 7: Configure and Update OpenVAS Feed:

Once logged in, you may need to configure and update the OpenVAS feed. Follow the on-screen instructions to accomplish this.

With these steps, you should have a functional installation of OpenVAS on your Windows machine using WSL. Keep in mind that this approach leverages a Linux environment within Windows, and while it provides OpenVAS functionality, the native experience may vary compared to running OpenVAS on a dedicated Linux system. Always refer to the official OpenVAS documentation and community resources for the latest updates and best practices.

2.2 Installation on Linux

Installing OpenVAS on a Linux system involves a series of steps to set up the necessary components for vulnerability scanning. The following guide outlines the installation process on a typical Linux distribution. For demonstration purposes, we'll use a Debian-based distribution (e.g., Ubuntu), but the steps may vary slightly depending on the specific distribution.

Prerequisites:

Update Package Lists:

sudo apt update && sudo apt upgrade -y

Install Required Dependencies:

sudo apt install -y wget curl gnupg

Installation Steps:

Step 1: Add the GPG Key:

wget -q -O - https://www.atomicorp.com/installers/atomic | sudo bash

Step 2: Install the OpenVAS Package:

sudo apt-get install -y openvas

Step 3: Start OpenVAS Services:

sudo systemctl start openvas-scanner
sudo systemctl start openvas-manager
sudo systemctl start openvas-gsa

Step 4: Enable Autostart (Optional):

To ensure OpenVAS starts automatically with your system:

sudo systemctl enable openvas-scanner
sudo systemctl enable openvas-manager
sudo systemctl enable openvas-gsa

Step 5: Access OpenVAS Web Interface:

Open a web browser and navigate to https://localhost:9392. Log in using the default credentials:

Username: admin
Password: admin

Step 6: Configure and Update OpenVAS Feed:

Upon logging in, you may need to configure and update the OpenVAS feed. Follow the on-screen instructions to accomplish this.

Step 7: Change Admin Password (Recommended):

Change the default admin password for security reasons:

sudo openvasmd --user=admin --new-password=<your_new_password>

With these steps, you should have a functional installation of OpenVAS on your Linux machine. The OpenVAS web interface provides a comprehensive platform for configuring scans, interpreting results, and managing vulnerability assessments. Always refer to the official OpenVAS documentation and community resources for the latest updates and best practices. Additionally, consider customizing the configuration based on your specific security requirements.

2.3 Initial Configuration Steps

After successfully installing OpenVAS on your system, there are several crucial initial configuration steps to ensure optimal performance, security, and usability. The following guide outlines key steps to configure OpenVAS and prepare it for effective vulnerability assessments.

1. Change Default Admin Password:

For security reasons, it's essential to change the default password for the admin user. Open a terminal and use the following command:

sudo openvasmd --user=admin --new-password=<your_new_password>

Replace <your_new_password> with a strong and secure password.

2. Update OpenVAS Feed:

Keep OpenVAS updated with the latest vulnerability information by updating the feed. This ensures that your vulnerability assessments are based on the most recent data. Run the following commands:

sudo greenbone-nvt-sync
sudo greenbone-scapdata-sync
sudo greenbone-certdata-sync

3. Configure Email Notifications (Optional):

If you want to receive email notifications for scan results or other important events, configure the email settings. Edit the OpenVAS configuration file:

sudo nano /etc/default/openvas-gsa

Find the line #GSA_EMAIL_CONFIG= and uncomment it by removing the #. Update the email settings accordingly. Save the file and restart the OpenVAS GSA service:

sudo systemctl restart openvas-gsa

4. Adjust Security Settings:

Consider adjusting security settings based on your organization's policies and requirements. OpenVAS has several security-related configuration files. Edit them as needed:

- **Scanner Configuration**: /etc/openvas/openvassd.conf
- **Manager Configuration**: /etc/openvas/openvasmd.conf
- **Greenbone Security Assistant (GSA) Configuration**: /etc/default/openvas-gsa

Make changes cautiously and refer to the official OpenVAS documentation for detailed explanations of each configuration option.

5. Create Additional Users (Optional):

If multiple individuals or teams will be using OpenVAS, consider creating additional users with specific roles and permissions. Use the following command to create a new user:

sudo openvasmd --create-user=<username> --role=<role>

Replace <username> with the desired username and <role> with the user's role (e.g., Admin, Manager, Scanner).

6. Schedule Regular Scans:

Automate vulnerability assessments by scheduling regular scans. This ensures that your systems are continuously monitored for vulnerabilities. Use the OpenVAS web interface to create and schedule new scans based on your organization's requirements.

7. Explore and Customize:

Explore the OpenVAS web interface and familiarize yourself with its features. Customize scan configurations, tweak preferences, and review the reporting options. OpenVAS provides extensive customization to tailor vulnerability assessments to your specific needs.

8. Check System Logs:

Regularly check system logs for any error messages or issues related to OpenVAS. The logs can provide valuable insights into the health and performance of the OpenVAS components.

9. Stay Informed:

Stay informed about updates, new features, and best practices for OpenVAS. Monitor the official OpenVAS documentation, community forums, and mailing lists for the latest information and security advisories.

These initial configuration steps are essential for ensuring that OpenVAS operates efficiently, securely, and in alignment with your organization's cybersecurity policies. Regularly revisit and update these configurations as your organization's needs evolve. Leveraging the full capabilities of OpenVAS requires ongoing engagement with the tool and the cybersecurity community to stay abreast of emerging threats and industry best practices.

2.4 User Account Management

Effective user account management is crucial in OpenVAS to ensure secure and controlled access to the vulnerability scanning platform. OpenVAS provides role-based access control, allowing administrators to define specific roles and permissions for each user. Here are the key user account management tasks in OpenVAS:

1. Create a New User:

To create a new user, use the following command:

sudo openvasmd --create-user=<username> --role=<role>

Replace <username> with the desired username and <role> with the user's role, such as Admin, Manager, or Scanner.

2. Set a Password for the User:

After creating a new user, set a password using the following command:

sudo openvasmd --user=<username> --new-password=<password>

Replace <username> with the username you created and <password> with a secure password.

3. List All Users:

To view a list of all users, use the following command:

sudo openvasmd --get-users

4. Modify User Roles:

If needed, you can modify the role assigned to a user. Use the following command:

sudo openvasmd --modify-user=<username> --role=<new_role>

Replace <username> with the username and <new_role> with the new role (e.g., Manager, Scanner).

5. Delete a User:

If a user is no longer needed, you can delete the user account using the following command:

sudo openvasmd --delete-user=<username>

Replace <username> with the username you want to delete.

6. Assign Scanners to Users (Optional):

In OpenVAS, scanners are associated with users. To assign scanners to a user, use the following command:

sudo openvasmd --modify-user=<username> --scanner=<scanner_id>

Replace <username> with the username and <scanner_id> with the ID of the scanner you want to assign.

7. Set User Preferences (Optional):

Users can have specific preferences configured. Use the following command to set user preferences:

sudo openvasmd --modify-user=<username>
--preferences='<preferences_json>'

Replace <username> with the username and <preferences_json> with a JSON-formatted string containing the desired preferences.

8. User Interface:

Apart from the command-line interface, you can also manage users through the OpenVAS web interface. Log in as an administrator and navigate to the "Users" section to add, modify, or delete users.

9. Audit User Activity:

Regularly audit user activity by checking logs and reports. This ensures that user actions are tracked, and any suspicious or unauthorized activities can be promptly identified and addressed.

10. Educate Users:

Provide training and documentation to users about their roles, responsibilities, and best practices when using OpenVAS. Educated users are more likely to follow security guidelines, enhancing the overall security posture.

User account management is a fundamental aspect of maintaining a secure and well-organized OpenVAS deployment. By following these user management tasks, administrators can establish a structured access control system, assign appropriate roles, and ensure that users are contributing effectively to the organization's vulnerability management efforts. Regularly review and update user accounts to align with changes in organizational structure and security requirements.

3. Navigating the OpenVAS Interface

As we venture deeper into the realm of cybersecurity preparedness, the efficacy of any tool lies not just in its existence but in the intuitive mastery of its interface. Chapter 3 serves as your compass in the exploration of the Open Vulnerability Assessment System (OpenVAS) interface—a digital cockpit that holds the key to uncovering vulnerabilities and fortifying your digital fortresses.

The Dashboard Unveiled

In the first subchapter, we embark on a guided tour through the OpenVAS dashboard. This digital command center provides a panoramic view of your cybersecurity landscape, displaying critical information and insights. Understanding the nuances of the dashboard is not merely about navigation; it's about gaining the situational awareness needed to make informed decisions in the face of evolving cyber threats.

Features and Functions Explored

Our journey continues as we delve into the diverse features and functions that form the backbone of OpenVAS. From scan configurations to report generation, every aspect of the tool plays a vital role in the vulnerability assessment process. The second subchapter equips you with the knowledge needed to harness these features effectively, empowering you to tailor OpenVAS to the specific needs of your cybersecurity strategy.

Customizing the Interface for Efficiency

Just as a skilled artisan hones their tools, cybersecurity professionals must customize their interfaces for optimal efficiency. In the final subchapter, we explore the various customization options within OpenVAS, allowing you to mold the interface to suit your workflow seamlessly. Efficiency in navigation not only saves time but also enhances the precision of your vulnerability assessments.

As Chapter 3 unfolds, you will not only navigate the OpenVAS interface but also comprehend its intricacies, unlocking the potential to wield this tool with finesse. Join us as we delve into the heart of OpenVAS, where the interface becomes more than a visual representation—it becomes a conduit to proactive cybersecurity.

3.1 Dashboard Overview

The OpenVAS dashboard provides a centralized and visual representation of the current state of your vulnerability management activities. It offers key insights into recent scan results, risk levels, and overall system health. Understanding the dashboard is essential for effectively monitoring and managing the security of your systems. Let's explore the main components and features of the OpenVAS dashboard:

1. Summary Metrics:

The dashboard typically displays summary metrics that provide a quick snapshot of the vulnerability landscape. Common metrics include:

- **Total Hosts**: The number of hosts in your network or environment.
- **Total Scans**: The overall count of vulnerability scans conducted.
- **High/Medium/Low/Critical Vulnerabilities**: The number of vulnerabilities categorized by severity levels.

These metrics give a high-level overview of the security posture and help in identifying trends or areas that require immediate attention.

2. Recent Scan Results:

A section of the dashboard is dedicated to displaying recent scan results. It may include:

- **Latest Scans**: Information about the most recent vulnerability scans conducted.
- **Scan Status**: The status of each scan, such as "Completed," "Running," or "Stopped."
- **Scan Duration**: The time taken for each scan to complete.

Reviewing recent scan results allows administrators to track the progress of ongoing scans and quickly identify any issues or improvements.

3. Risk Distribution:

The distribution of vulnerabilities based on risk levels is often presented graphically. This visual representation helps in understanding the distribution of high, medium, low, and critical vulnerabilities across the environment.

- **Pie Chart or Bar Graphs**: Graphical elements that illustrate the percentage or count of vulnerabilities in each risk category.

This visual representation aids in prioritizing remediation efforts by focusing on the most critical vulnerabilities first.

4. System Health:

The health of the OpenVAS system itself is crucial for reliable vulnerability assessments. The dashboard may include indicators or information related to:

- **Database Status**: Indicating whether the vulnerability database is up-to-date.
- **Scanner and Manager Status**: Providing insights into the operational status of key components.
- **Feed Status**: Confirming the current status of the vulnerability feed and whether updates are being received.

A healthy system ensures accurate and timely vulnerability assessments.

5. User Activity:

Some dashboards include a section on user activity, showing:

- **Recent User Logins**: Listing the usernames and timestamps of recent logins.
- **User Actions**: Highlighting significant actions taken by users, such as starting or stopping scans.

Monitoring user activity is essential for security and audit purposes, helping to identify any unauthorized or suspicious actions.

6. Customizable Widgets:

Many modern OpenVAS interfaces allow users to customize their dashboards by adding or removing widgets. Common widgets include:

- **Quick Scan Buttons**: Providing one-click access to commonly used scan configurations.
- **Top Vulnerabilities**: Displaying the most prevalent vulnerabilities in the environment.

- **Graphs and Charts**: Visualizing trends or patterns in vulnerability data.

Customization empowers users to tailor the dashboard to their specific needs and priorities.

7. Actionable Insights:

An effective OpenVAS dashboard provides actionable insights. This means that, beyond displaying information, the dashboard should offer links or options to directly perform actions such as initiating scans, reviewing detailed reports, or addressing specific vulnerabilities.

The OpenVAS dashboard is a central hub for monitoring and managing the vulnerability landscape. By regularly reviewing the dashboard, security administrators can make informed decisions, prioritize remediation efforts, and ensure the ongoing security of their systems. Understanding the various components and metrics presented on the dashboard is key to harnessing the full potential of OpenVAS for proactive vulnerability management.

3.2 Key Features and Functions

OpenVAS (Open Vulnerability Assessment System) is a powerful tool designed to identify and manage vulnerabilities in computer systems. Understanding its key features and functions is crucial for effective vulnerability management. Here are the core aspects that make OpenVAS a comprehensive solution:

1. Scalable Architecture:

OpenVAS is designed with scalability in mind, making it suitable for environments of varying sizes. Whether you are securing a small business network or a large enterprise infrastructure, OpenVAS can scale to meet the demands of diverse organizations.

2. Comprehensive Vulnerability Scanning:

OpenVAS performs comprehensive vulnerability scans across a wide range of targets, including servers, network devices, and applications. It identifies vulnerabilities in operating systems, software, configurations, and other potential security weaknesses.

3. Extensive Vulnerability Database:

OpenVAS relies on an extensive and regularly updated vulnerability database. This database includes information about known vulnerabilities, allowing OpenVAS to compare the current state of systems against a vast repository of security-related data.

4. Categorization of Vulnerabilities:

Vulnerabilities identified by OpenVAS are categorized based on severity levels, helping organizations prioritize remediation efforts. Common severity levels include critical, high, medium, and low. This categorization assists in focusing resources on addressing the most critical issues first.

5. Authenticated Scanning:

OpenVAS supports authenticated scanning, allowing it to assess systems with user credentials. Authenticated scans provide a more in-depth analysis, uncovering vulnerabilities that might be missed in non-authenticated scans. This is especially valuable for identifying configuration issues and potential exploits.

6. Customizable Scanning Policies:

Users can define and customize scanning policies based on their specific requirements. This flexibility enables organizations to tailor vulnerability assessments to their unique environments, considering factors such as compliance requirements, network architecture, and risk tolerance.

7. Scheduled Scans:

OpenVAS supports the scheduling of vulnerability scans. Organizations can automate regular scans, ensuring continuous monitoring and timely identification of new vulnerabilities. Scheduled scans contribute to proactive vulnerability management and reduce the window of exposure to potential threats.

8. Web-Based User Interface:

OpenVAS provides a user-friendly web-based interface, known as the Greenbone Security Assistant (GSA). The GSA allows users to interact with OpenVAS, configure scans, view reports, and manage vulnerabilities through an intuitive and accessible platform.

9. Role-Based Access Control (RBAC):

Role-Based Access Control is implemented in OpenVAS, allowing administrators to define roles and assign specific permissions to users. This fine-grained access control ensures that users have appropriate privileges based on their responsibilities within the organization.

10. Reporting and Documentation:

OpenVAS generates detailed reports that provide insights into scan results, identified vulnerabilities, and recommendations for remediation. Reports can be customized and exported in various formats, facilitating communication with stakeholders and supporting compliance requirements.

11. Integration Capabilities:

OpenVAS can be integrated into broader cybersecurity ecosystems. It supports integration with Security Information and Event Management (SIEM) systems, allowing organizations to correlate vulnerability data with other security events for a holistic view of the threat landscape.

12. Community and Support:

OpenVAS benefits from a vibrant community of users and contributors. Community support forums, documentation, and collaborative development contribute to the ongoing improvement and evolution of the tool. Commercial support options are also available for organizations that require additional assistance.

13. Regular Updates and Feeds:

OpenVAS relies on regular updates and feeds to stay current with the latest vulnerabilities and security information. Users can synchronize the OpenVAS feeds to ensure that the tool has access to the most up-to-date data for effective vulnerability assessments.

OpenVAS combines a robust set of features with a user-friendly interface, making it a versatile and widely used tool for vulnerability assessment and management. Its scalability, customization options, and integration capabilities contribute to its effectiveness in helping organizations identify and address security vulnerabilities proactively. Whether used by cybersecurity professionals, system administrators, or compliance officers, OpenVAS plays a crucial role in fortifying digital defenses against evolving cyber threats.

3.3 Customizing the Interface

Customizing the OpenVAS interface is a valuable aspect of tailoring the user experience to meet specific organizational needs and preferences. The Greenbone Security Assistant (GSA) serves as the web-based interface for OpenVAS, and it provides various customization options. Here are key ways to customize the OpenVAS interface:

1. Theme Selection:

The GSA interface offers different themes to choose from, allowing users to select a color scheme that suits their preferences. Themes can enhance readability and aesthetics. To change the theme, navigate to the GSA interface, click on the user icon, and select "Preferences." Under the "General" tab, choose the desired theme.

2. Dashboard Widgets:

Customizing the dashboard with relevant widgets enhances usability. Users can add, remove, or rearrange widgets based on their preferences. Common widgets include quick scan buttons, recent scan results, and vulnerability distribution graphs. To customize the dashboard, click on the "Customize" button on the dashboard page.

3. Report Templates:

Users can create custom report templates to generate reports with specific content and formatting. This is particularly useful for aligning reports with organizational standards or compliance requirements. To create a report template, navigate to the "Reports" section in the GSA interface and select "Report Formats."

4. Scan Configuration:

Customizing scan configurations allows users to define specific parameters for vulnerability scans. This includes setting scan targets, configuring scan policies, and defining scan schedules. Access the "Scans" section in the GSA interface to create or modify scan configurations based on organizational requirements.

5. User Preferences:

Users can personalize their experience by configuring individual preferences. This includes settings related to language, time zone, and email notifications. To adjust user preferences, click on the user icon in the GSA interface and select "Preferences."

6. Filtering and Sorting:

Customizing the way information is filtered and sorted in tables and lists can improve data analysis. In various sections of the GSA interface, users can often find options to filter and sort information based on specific criteria.

7. Target Groups:

Organizing scan targets into groups, known as target groups, facilitates efficient management. Users can create target groups based on criteria such as location, department, or system type. This helps streamline vulnerability assessments. Manage target groups through the "Targets" section in the GSA interface.

8. Role-Based Access Control (RBAC):

Adjusting role-based access control settings enables administrators to define roles and permissions for users. This customization ensures that users have appropriate levels of access based on their responsibilities. Manage RBAC settings under the "Users" section in the GSA interface.

9. Alerts and Notifications:

Configure alerts and notifications to stay informed about critical events, scan results, or system health. Users can set up email notifications or integrate with other alerting mechanisms. Configure alert settings in the GSA interface under "Preferences."

10. Language Preferences:

OpenVAS supports multiple languages, allowing users to select their preferred language for the interface. This is especially beneficial for global teams. Adjust language preferences in the user settings under "Preferences."

Customizing the OpenVAS interface enhances user satisfaction, productivity, and the overall effectiveness of vulnerability management efforts. By tailoring the interface to organizational workflows and preferences, users can optimize their experience with OpenVAS, leading to more efficient vulnerability assessments and remediation processes. Regularly reviewing and adjusting these customizations ensures that OpenVAS aligns with evolving organizational requirements.

4. Target Identification and Scoping

In the realm of cybersecurity, precision is paramount. As we continue our expedition through the intricacies of OpenVAS, Chapter 4 beckons us to the critical phase of vulnerability assessment—target identification and scoping. Just as a skilled archer focuses on the bullseye, cybersecurity professionals must hone their abilities to pinpoint vulnerabilities with accuracy and diligence.

Defining the Scope of Assessment

The first subchapter lays the groundwork by unraveling the concept of scoping in vulnerability assessments. Understanding the boundaries of your assessment is not only a strategic decision but a tactical necessity. From defining the systems in scope to establishing the parameters of your assessment, this section provides the compass needed to navigate the vast landscape of potential vulnerabilities.

Identifying Target Systems and Networks

Our journey then shifts to the second subchapter, where we explore the art of identifying target systems and networks. This step is the foundation upon which the entire vulnerability assessment process is built. Through meticulous methodologies and scanning techniques, you will gain the insights required to identify and catalog the digital assets that demand your scrutiny.

Scanning Methodologies and Techniques

In the final subchapter, we delve into the diverse scanning methodologies and techniques available within OpenVAS. Just as a detective employs various methods to solve a case, a cybersecurity professional must leverage different scanning approaches to uncover vulnerabilities effectively. From comprehensive full scans to targeted and stealthy approaches, you will learn to wield OpenVAS as your investigative ally.

As Chapter 4 unfolds, you will not only grasp the importance of meticulous target identification and scoping but also acquire the skills needed to execute these crucial steps with finesse. Join us in the exploration of precision within OpenVAS, where every scan is a step closer to a more secure digital landscape.

4.1 Defining the Scope of Assessment

Defining the scope of assessment is a critical step in conducting effective vulnerability assessments with OpenVAS. The scope outlines the specific systems, networks, and assets that will be included in the assessment. Properly defining the scope helps focus the assessment efforts, ensures comprehensive coverage, and facilitates more accurate and actionable results. Here are key considerations for defining the scope of assessment in OpenVAS:

1. Identify Target Systems:

Begin by identifying the systems, networks, and assets that you want to include in the vulnerability assessment. This may involve creating an inventory of all the assets within your organization, including servers, workstations, network devices, and other critical infrastructure components.

2. Define IP Ranges:

Specify the IP ranges associated with the target systems. OpenVAS uses IP addresses to identify and scan target systems. Clearly define the ranges to ensure that all relevant systems are included in the assessment.

3. Consider Network Segments:

If your organization has different network segments or VLANs, consider whether all segments should be included in the assessment or if specific segments need special attention. This is particularly important for larger organizations with complex network architectures.

4. Inclusion and Exclusion Criteria:

Establish criteria for including or excluding systems from the assessment. For example, you may choose to exclude certain systems due to critical business functions, sensitivity, or specific compliance requirements. Conversely, you may want to ensure the inclusion of critical infrastructure components.

5. Asset Classification:

Classify assets based on their criticality to the business. Assigning a risk or criticality level to each asset helps prioritize remediation efforts. OpenVAS allows users to tag assets with labels for better organization and reporting.

6. Authentication Considerations:

Decide whether authenticated scans will be performed. Authenticated scans provide deeper insights into the security posture of systems by scanning with user credentials. Ensure that the scope includes systems for which authentication is feasible and desirable.

7. Compliance Requirements:

Consider any compliance requirements or industry standards that impact the scope of the assessment. Certain regulations or standards may mandate the inclusion of specific systems or the evaluation of particular security controls.

8. Collaborate with Stakeholders:

Collaborate with relevant stakeholders, including system owners, IT administrators, and security personnel, to ensure that the scope aligns with organizational objectives and priorities. Gathering input from various departments helps create a more comprehensive and accurate scope.

9. Documentation:

Document the scope of the assessment in a clear and detailed manner. This documentation should be accessible to all relevant parties and serve as a reference throughout the assessment process. Include details such as IP ranges, asset classifications, and any specific considerations.

10. Review and Update:

Regularly review and update the scope to reflect changes in the organization's infrastructure, business processes, or security requirements. The dynamic nature of IT environments necessitates ongoing assessment and adjustment of the scope.

Defining the scope of assessment is foundational to a successful vulnerability assessment with OpenVAS. A well-defined scope sets the boundaries for the assessment, ensuring that resources are focused on the most critical systems and potential vulnerabilities. By following a systematic and collaborative approach to scoping, organizations can maximize the effectiveness of their vulnerability management efforts.

4.2 Identifying Target Systems and Networks

Identifying target systems and networks is a crucial step in preparing for a successful OpenVAS vulnerability assessment. This process involves determining the specific assets within your organization that will be subjected to the assessment. Here are key steps and considerations for identifying target systems and networks:

1. Create an Asset Inventory:

Develop a comprehensive inventory of all assets within your organization. This includes servers, workstations, network devices, databases, and any other systems that are part of your IT infrastructure. The asset inventory serves as the foundation for identifying targets.

2. Collaborate with IT and Security Teams:

Engage with IT administrators, system owners, and security personnel to gather insights into the organization's infrastructure. Collaborative discussions can help identify critical systems, network segments, and potential vulnerabilities that require attention.

3. Network Topology Analysis:

Understand the organization's network topology. Identify network segments, subnets, and the interconnectivity between systems. Recognize areas with high traffic, sensitive information flow, or critical functions. This analysis informs the scoping process.

4. IP Address Ranges:

Define the IP address ranges associated with the target systems. OpenVAS utilizes IP addresses to conduct vulnerability scans.

Specify IP ranges accurately to ensure that all relevant systems are included. This may involve including specific subnets or ranges associated with different departments or locations.

5. Segmentation and VLANs:

Consider network segmentation and VLANs (Virtual Local Area Networks) within the organization. Determine whether systems within different segments or VLANs should be included in the assessment. For larger organizations, this is particularly important in ensuring comprehensive coverage.

6. Business Criticality:

Assess the criticality of each asset to the business. Classify systems based on their importance to organizational operations. Critical systems may include those supporting core business functions, storing sensitive data, or hosting mission-critical applications.

7. Compliance Requirements:

Take into account any compliance requirements or industry standards that mandate specific systems to be included in the assessment. Compliance frameworks often dictate the need for regular vulnerability assessments, and the scope should align with these regulatory obligations.

8. Authentication Considerations:

Consider whether authenticated scans will be conducted. Authenticated scans, which involve scanning with user credentials, provide a more in-depth analysis of the security posture of systems. Identify systems for which authentication is feasible and desirable.

9. Document the Scope:

Document the identified target systems and networks in a clear and detailed manner. Include information such as IP address ranges, network segments, and any special considerations. This documentation serves as a reference throughout the vulnerability assessment process.

10. Review and Update Regularly:

The IT environment is dynamic, with changes occurring regularly. Review and update the list of target systems and networks on a regular basis. Changes in infrastructure, system configurations, or business priorities may necessitate adjustments to the scope.

Identifying target systems and networks is a fundamental step that shapes the success of an OpenVAS vulnerability assessment. By leveraging collaboration, thorough analysis, and documentation, organizations can establish a well-defined scope that ensures the assessment addresses critical assets and potential vulnerabilities within the IT landscape. Regular reviews and updates to the scope contribute to the agility and effectiveness of the vulnerability management process.

4.3 Scanning Methodologies and Techniques

Effective scanning methodologies and techniques are essential for maximizing the value of a vulnerability assessment with OpenVAS. OpenVAS employs a variety of scanning techniques to identify vulnerabilities and security issues within target systems. Understanding these methodologies helps users configure scans appropriately and interpret results accurately. Here are key scanning methodologies and techniques in OpenVAS:

1. Network Scanning:

Network scanning involves probing and examining the network to identify live hosts, open ports, and network services. OpenVAS utilizes network scanning to discover systems within the defined scope. This is the initial phase of a vulnerability assessment, providing a foundation for subsequent detailed scans.

2. Port Scanning:

Port scanning is the process of identifying open ports on target systems. OpenVAS performs port scanning to determine which ports are accessible and potentially vulnerable to exploitation. Information about open ports assists in narrowing down the focus of vulnerability scans.

3. Service Version Detection:

Once open ports are identified, OpenVAS performs service version detection to determine the specific versions of services running on those ports. Knowing the service versions is crucial for accurately identifying known vulnerabilities associated with specific software versions.

4. Vulnerability Detection:

Vulnerability detection is the core function of OpenVAS. It systematically scans target systems for known vulnerabilities based on its extensive vulnerability database. OpenVAS uses a signature-based approach, matching known patterns associated with vulnerabilities to identify potential security issues.

5. Authenticated Scanning:

Authenticated scanning involves conducting vulnerability assessments with user credentials. This method provides deeper insights into the security posture of systems by allowing OpenVAS to access system information that is not available during non-authenticated scans. Authenticated scanning is particularly valuable for identifying configuration issues and potential exploits.

6. Compliance Checks:

OpenVAS includes compliance checks to assess whether systems adhere to specific security standards or compliance requirements. This may involve checking configurations against industry standards such as CIS benchmarks or compliance frameworks like PCI DSS.

7. Web Application Scanning:

OpenVAS supports scanning of web applications to identify vulnerabilities such as SQL injection, cross-site scripting (XSS), and other web-related security issues. This extends the assessment beyond traditional network and system vulnerabilities to cover potential weaknesses in web applications.

8. Database Scanning:

For environments with databases, OpenVAS can scan database systems to identify vulnerabilities or misconfigurations. Database scanning includes checks for common issues in database security, such as weak authentication, missing patches, or excessive permissions.

9. Bruteforce Attacks:

OpenVAS can simulate bruteforce attacks to test the strength of authentication mechanisms. This involves attempting to gain unauthorized access by systematically trying different usernames and passwords. Simulating bruteforce attacks helps identify weak or easily guessable credentials.

10. Incremental Scanning:

Incremental scanning focuses on changes since the last scan. Instead of scanning the entire network, OpenVAS identifies and scans systems that have been modified or added. Incremental scanning is more resource-efficient and suitable for environments with frequent changes.

OpenVAS employs a diverse set of scanning methodologies and techniques to comprehensively assess the security posture of target systems. The combination of network scanning, vulnerability detection, compliance checks, and specialized scans for web applications and databases enables organizations to identify and remediate security issues effectively. By understanding these methodologies, users can configure OpenVAS scans to align with their specific security requirements and priorities. Regularly updating the OpenVAS vulnerability database ensures that the tool remains effective in identifying the latest security threats.

5. Vulnerability Scanning with OpenVAS

In the labyrinth of cybersecurity, where hidden vulnerabilities lie dormant, the role of a vigilant sentinel comes to life in Chapter 5. This segment of our journey takes us deep into the heart of OpenVAS, where the art of vulnerability scanning becomes a potent weapon in the arsenal of cybersecurity defense.

Configuring Scans for Precision

The first subchapter is a hands-on exploration of configuring vulnerability scans with precision. From defining scan policies to selecting targets and setting parameters, this section equips you with the knowledge needed to tailor OpenVAS scans to your specific cybersecurity requirements. Here, we unravel the intricacies of customization, ensuring that every scan is a targeted expedition into the vulnerabilities that may lurk within your digital domain.

Launching Scans: The Tactical Deployment

With configurations in place, we move to the second subchapter, where the tactical deployment of scans takes center stage. Launching a scan is more than just a button click; it's a strategic maneuver that requires an understanding of timing, context, and the potential impact on your digital landscape. Here, we guide you through the process of initiating scans, ensuring that your OpenVAS deployment is not only effective but conducted with precision.

Understanding Scan Results: Decrypting the Findings

As the scans unfold, the third subchapter delves into the crucial task of understanding scan results. Like deciphering a complex code, interpreting the findings of a vulnerability scan requires a keen eye and a strategic mindset. We explore the intricacies of OpenVAS reports, helping you discern critical vulnerabilities from false alarms and providing you with the insights needed to prioritize remediation efforts effectively.

Dealing with False Positives and Negatives

The final subchapter addresses the nuanced task of handling false positives and negatives. In the ever-evolving landscape of cybersecurity, not every alert is a red flag, and not every vulnerability is apparent. Here, we guide you through the process of distinguishing false positives from genuine threats and strategizing the most effective responses to ensure your defenses remain resilient.

As Chapter 5 unfolds, you will not only navigate the terrain of vulnerability scanning but also hone your skills in configuring, launching, and deciphering the results of OpenVAS scans. Join us as we delve into the tactical aspects of cybersecurity defense, where precision and insight become your allies in the ongoing battle against digital threats.

5.1 Configuring Scans

Configuring scans in OpenVAS is a crucial step to ensure that vulnerability assessments are tailored to the specific requirements and priorities of your organization. The configuration process involves defining scan parameters, selecting targets, and specifying options that align with your security goals. Here's a step-by-step guide to configuring scans in OpenVAS:

1. Access the Greenbone Security Assistant (GSA):

Open a web browser and access the Greenbone Security Assistant by navigating to the OpenVAS web interface. The default URL is typically https://localhost:9392. Log in with your credentials.

2. Navigate to the "Scans" Section:

In the GSA interface, navigate to the "Scans" section. This is where you can manage and configure your vulnerability scans.

3. Create a New Scan:

Click on the "Create" button or a similar option to initiate the creation of a new scan.

4. Provide a Descriptive Name:

Give your scan a descriptive and meaningful name. This helps in identifying and managing multiple scans, especially in environments with various ongoing assessments.

5. Select Targets:

Specify the target systems or networks that you want to include in the scan. This can be done by entering IP addresses, defining IP ranges, or selecting predefined target groups.

6. Choose Scan Configurations:

Select the scan configurations that align with your assessment goals. OpenVAS provides predefined scan configurations such as "Full and Fast," "Full and Fast Ultimate," "Discovery," and others. Choose the configuration that best fits your requirements.

7. Configure Scan Options:

Adjust scan options based on your preferences. This includes settings such as the maximum number of concurrently scanned hosts, the maximum number of simultaneous tests, and the scan timeout. Fine-tune these options to balance scan speed and resource usage.

8. Authentication Settings (If Applicable):

If you are conducting authenticated scans, provide the necessary authentication credentials. This may include usernames, passwords, and other authentication details required for accessing target systems with sufficient privileges.

9. Schedule the Scan (Optional):

You have the option to schedule the scan for a specific date and time. Scheduling scans is beneficial for automating assessments and ensuring that vulnerability assessments are conducted regularly.

10. Configure Advanced Options:

Explore advanced options based on your specific needs. This may include adjusting settings related to performance, reporting, or specific scan plugins. Advanced options provide additional customization for fine-tuning the scan process.

11. Save and Launch the Scan:

Once you have configured the scan to your satisfaction, save the settings and initiate the scan. Depending on your configuration, the scan may start immediately or at the scheduled time.

12. Monitor and Review Results:

Monitor the progress of the scan in real-time through the OpenVAS interface. Once the scan is complete, review the results and reports generated by OpenVAS. Pay attention to identified vulnerabilities, severity levels, and recommended actions.

13. Adjust and Iterate:

Based on the scan results, iterate and adjust your scanning configurations as needed. Refine the scope, modify scan options, or include/exclude specific targets based on the insights gained from the assessment.

Configuring scans in OpenVAS is a dynamic process that requires consideration of your organization's unique requirements, network architecture, and security goals. Regularly reviewing and refining scan configurations ensures that vulnerability assessments remain effective in identifying and addressing security issues. The flexibility and customization options provided by OpenVAS empower users to adapt their scanning strategies to evolving security challenges.

5.2 Launching Scans

Launching scans in OpenVAS is the culmination of the configuration process and initiates the vulnerability assessment. The steps below guide you through the process of launching scans using the Greenbone Security Assistant (GSA), the web-based interface for OpenVAS:

1. Access the Greenbone Security Assistant (GSA):

Open your web browser and access the Greenbone Security Assistant by navigating to the OpenVAS web interface. Use the appropriate URL, typically https://localhost:9392. Log in with your credentials.

2. Navigate to the "Scans" Section:

In the GSA interface, navigate to the "Scans" section. This is where you manage and monitor your vulnerability scans.

3. Select the Scan Configuration:

Choose the scan configuration that you previously created or select a predefined configuration that aligns with your assessment goals. Ensure that the configuration includes the appropriate target systems and scan options.

4. Verify Settings:

Review the scan settings to confirm that they align with your requirements. Double-check the selected targets, authentication settings (if applicable), and any advanced options you may have configured.

5. Click on "Launch Scan":

Locate the "Launch Scan" or similar button to initiate the vulnerability scan. Click on it to start the assessment process. Depending on your configuration, the scan may start immediately or be scheduled for a specific date and time.

6. Monitor Scan Progress:

After launching the scan, monitor its progress in real-time through the OpenVAS interface. You can view details such as the number of scanned hosts, current status, and any identified vulnerabilities. The interface provides insights into the ongoing assessment.

7. Review Scan Results:

Once the scan is complete, review the results and reports generated by OpenVAS. The results include information about identified vulnerabilities, their severity levels, and recommendations for remediation. Take note of critical issues that require immediate attention.

8. Export Reports (Optional):

If needed, export scan reports for further analysis or documentation. OpenVAS allows you to export reports in various formats, such as PDF or XML. This is useful for sharing results with stakeholders or incorporating them into broader security documentation.

9. Address Identified Vulnerabilities:

Act on the identified vulnerabilities by prioritizing and addressing them based on their severity levels. Develop a remediation plan and implement necessary security measures to mitigate the risks associated with the vulnerabilities.

10. Iterate and Refine:

Based on the insights gained from the scan results, iterate and refine your scanning configurations. Adjust the scope, modify scan options, or include/exclude specific targets as needed. Regularly updating and optimizing your scanning approach enhances the effectiveness of vulnerability assessments.

11. Schedule Regular Scans:

For ongoing vulnerability management, consider scheduling regular scans to ensure that your organization's security posture is continuously assessed. Regular scans help identify new vulnerabilities introduced by system changes or updates.

Launching scans in OpenVAS is a pivotal step in proactively managing the security of your IT infrastructure. The ability to configure, launch, and analyze scans provides organizations with a powerful tool for identifying and addressing vulnerabilities. By integrating regular vulnerability assessments into your cybersecurity practices, you can stay ahead of potential threats and enhance the overall resilience of your systems.

5.3 Understanding Scan Results

Understanding scan results is crucial for extracting actionable insights from vulnerability assessments conducted with OpenVAS. The scan results provide information about identified vulnerabilities, their severity levels, and recommendations for remediation. Here's a guide to help you interpret and navigate through the scan results in OpenVAS:

1. Access the Greenbone Security Assistant (GSA):

Open your web browser and log in to the Greenbone Security Assistant, which serves as the web-based interface for OpenVAS. Navigate to the "Scans" section to find the list of completed scans.

2. Select the Completed Scan:

Locate and select the completed scan for which you want to view the results. The scan list typically includes details such as the scan name, start time, and status.

3. View Summary Metrics:

The scan summary provides high-level metrics indicating the overall status and findings of the assessment. Key metrics may include the total number of hosts scanned, vulnerabilities identified, and an overview of vulnerabilities by severity level.

4. Explore the Vulnerabilities Tab:

Navigate to the "Vulnerabilities" tab or a similar section to view the detailed list of identified vulnerabilities. Each vulnerability is listed with information such as its name, severity level, and a brief description. Pay attention to critical and high-severity vulnerabilities.

5. Severity Levels:

Vulnerabilities are categorized into severity levels, typically ranging from critical to low. Understand the significance of each severity level:

- **Critical**: Represents vulnerabilities that pose a severe and immediate threat. Immediate remediation is often necessary.
- **High**: Indicates significant vulnerabilities that should be addressed promptly.
- **Medium**: Represents moderate-level vulnerabilities that require attention.

Low: Denotes lower-risk vulnerabilities that may be addressed based on organizational priorities.

6. Detailed Vulnerability Information:

Click on individual vulnerabilities to access more detailed information. This includes a comprehensive description of the vulnerability, potential impact, and recommended actions for remediation. Consider the context of your organization and the affected systems when evaluating the severity and impact of each vulnerability.

7. Review Affected Hosts:

For each vulnerability, review the list of affected hosts. Identify which systems are impacted by a particular vulnerability, as this information guides remediation efforts and helps prioritize actions.

8. Verify False Positives:

Evaluate whether any identified vulnerabilities are false positives. Sometimes, scan results may flag issues that are not actual vulnerabilities. Verify findings by cross-referencing with system configurations and other relevant information.

9. Generate Reports:

If needed, generate detailed reports for documentation and reporting purposes. OpenVAS allows you to export reports in various formats, such as PDF or XML. Reports are useful for sharing scan results with stakeholders, compliance auditors, or management.

10. Prioritize Remediation:

Prioritize remediation efforts based on the severity and potential impact of vulnerabilities. Develop a remediation plan that addresses critical and high-severity issues first, followed by medium and low-severity vulnerabilities.

11. Repeat Scans:

For ongoing vulnerability management, repeat scans regularly to identify new vulnerabilities and assess the effectiveness of remediation efforts. Regular scanning helps maintain an up-to-date understanding of the security posture of your systems.

12. Collaborate with Teams:

Share scan results and collaborate with relevant teams, including system administrators, IT personnel, and security teams. Effective communication ensures that remediation efforts are coordinated and aligned with organizational priorities.

Understanding scan results is pivotal for turning vulnerability assessments into actionable improvements in your organization's security posture. By systematically reviewing, prioritizing, and addressing vulnerabilities, you can enhance the resilience of your systems against potential threats. Regularly iterating through the vulnerability management process ensures that your organization stays proactive in addressing evolving security challenges.

5.4 Dealing with False Positives and Negatives

False positives and false negatives are common challenges in vulnerability assessments, and addressing them is crucial for the accuracy and effectiveness of the security testing process. Here's a guide on how to deal with false positives and negatives in OpenVAS:

Dealing with False Positives:

False positives occur when OpenVAS incorrectly identifies a non-vulnerability as a security issue. Managing false positives is essential to prevent unnecessary remediation efforts and ensure that resources are focused on genuine security risks.

Review Vulnerability Descriptions:

Carefully read the detailed descriptions of identified vulnerabilities. Ensure that you understand the nature of each vulnerability and its potential impact.

Check System Configurations:

Verify the configurations of the systems flagged with vulnerabilities. False positives may arise if OpenVAS misinterprets certain configurations. Cross-reference the findings with system documentation and configurations.

Update OpenVAS Plugins:

Regularly update the OpenVAS vulnerability database and plugins. New updates may include improved detection mechanisms and corrections for previously identified false positives.

Customize Scan Policies:

Adjust scan policies and configurations to reduce false positives. Fine-tune settings based on the specific characteristics of your organization's IT environment.

Validate Findings Through Manual Testing:

Conduct manual testing to validate the findings of OpenVAS. Manual testing can help confirm whether a flagged vulnerability is a false positive or a genuine issue.

Provide Feedback to OpenVAS Community:

If you encounter persistent false positives, consider providing feedback to the OpenVAS community. This collaborative approach helps improve the accuracy of vulnerability detection over time.

Dealing with False Negatives:

False negatives occur when OpenVAS fails to identify an actual vulnerability, leading to a potential security gap. Addressing false negatives is crucial to ensure that all relevant security risks are identified and mitigated.

Perform Additional Manual Testing:

Conduct additional manual testing to supplement automated scans. Manual testing can uncover vulnerabilities that may be missed by automated tools, addressing potential false negatives.

Verify Scan Configurations:

Review and verify scan configurations to ensure that the scanning policies are appropriate for your environment. Adjust settings to increase coverage and accuracy.

Check Authentication Settings:

If applicable, ensure that authenticated scanning is configured correctly. Authenticated scans provide deeper insights into the security posture of systems and may help uncover vulnerabilities that are not visible in non-authenticated scans.

Explore Specialized Scans:

Consider using specialized scans for specific types of vulnerabilities, such as web application scans or database scans. Specialized scans can address vulnerabilities that may be outside the scope of a general assessment.

Evaluate Patch Levels:

Verify the patch levels of systems to ensure that OpenVAS is not missing vulnerabilities that have known patches. Outdated systems may have vulnerabilities that can be addressed through patching.

Collaborate with Security Teams:

Collaborate with your organization's security teams to share insights and experiences. Security professionals may provide valuable input into areas that automated tools might overlook.

Regularly Update OpenVAS:

Keep OpenVAS and its plugins up to date to benefit from the latest vulnerability signatures and detection capabilities. Regular updates improve the tool's ability to identify both known and emerging vulnerabilities.

Effectively dealing with false positives and negatives requires a combination of technical expertise, collaboration, and continuous improvement. By refining scan configurations, conducting manual testing, and staying engaged with the cybersecurity community, you can enhance the accuracy of vulnerability assessments conducted with OpenVAS. Regularly reviewing and updating your approach to address false positives and negatives contributes to a more robust and reliable vulnerability management process.

6. Interpreting Scan Reports

In the intricate dance between cybersecurity threats and vigilant defense, information is not merely data—it's intelligence. Chapter 6 thrusts us into the realm of comprehension, where the art of interpreting OpenVAS scan reports transforms raw findings into actionable insights. As we dissect the results of our vulnerability assessments, the true mastery of cybersecurity unfolds.

Analyzing OpenVAS Reports: The Detective's Toolkit

The initial subchapter unveils the detective's toolkit for analyzing OpenVAS reports. Much like a detective scrutinizing evidence to solve a case, we guide you through the myriad elements within a report. From severity levels to vulnerability details, understanding this toolkit is essential for prioritizing remediation efforts and crafting a strategic defense.

Prioritizing Identified Vulnerabilities: The Art of Triage

With a plethora of vulnerabilities at your fingertips, the second subchapter introduces the art of triage—prioritizing identified vulnerabilities based on their criticality and potential impact. Here, we provide a framework for making informed decisions, ensuring that your cybersecurity efforts are focused on addressing the most significant threats first.

Generating Actionable Insights: From Knowledge to Defense

The final subchapter bridges the gap between knowledge and action. Information alone is not enough; it's the transformation of insights into action that fortifies your digital defenses. We explore strategies for translating OpenVAS scan reports into actionable steps, fostering a proactive cybersecurity posture within your organization.

As Chapter 6 unfolds, you will not only unravel the intricacies of OpenVAS scan reports but also acquire the skills needed to convert findings into proactive defense measures. Join us in the journey of interpretation, where every insight gained is a step closer to a fortified cybersecurity landscape.

6.1 Analyzing OpenVAS Reports

Analyzing OpenVAS reports is a crucial step in extracting meaningful insights from vulnerability assessments and making informed decisions regarding security improvements. OpenVAS provides detailed reports that highlight identified vulnerabilities, their severity levels, and recommended remediation actions. Here's a guide on how to effectively analyze OpenVAS reports:

1. Access the Greenbone Security Assistant (GSA):

Open your web browser and log in to the Greenbone Security Assistant, the web-based interface for OpenVAS. Navigate to the "Reports" section, where you can find and manage your vulnerability assessment reports.

2. Select the Relevant Report:

Locate and select the report that corresponds to the vulnerability assessment you want to analyze. Reports are typically organized by scan date, allowing you to choose the most recent or relevant assessment.

3. Review Executive Summary:

Start by reviewing the executive summary section of the report. This provides a high-level overview of the assessment, including the number of vulnerabilities identified, their distribution by severity, and a summary of the top issues.

4. Examine Vulnerability Details:

Navigate to the section that provides detailed information about identified vulnerabilities. Each vulnerability is listed with its name, severity level, and a brief description. Click on individual vulnerabilities to access more in-depth details.

5. Severity Levels:

Pay close attention to the severity levels assigned to each vulnerability. Severity levels, such as critical, high, medium, and low, help prioritize remediation efforts based on the potential impact of the vulnerabilities.

6. Affected Hosts:

Review the list of affected hosts for each vulnerability. Identify which systems are impacted, and consider the potential risk associated with vulnerabilities on critical or high-value assets.

7. Check for False Positives:

Verify whether any identified vulnerabilities are false positives. Cross-reference the findings with system configurations, and use your knowledge of the organization's IT environment to distinguish between genuine vulnerabilities and false positives.

8. Evaluate Recommendations:

For each vulnerability, assess the recommended remediation actions provided by OpenVAS. Consider the feasibility and impact of implementing these recommendations, and prioritize actions based on organizational risk tolerance and policies.

9. Generate Trend Analysis:

If your organization conducts regular vulnerability assessments, generate trend analyses to identify patterns over time. This helps track improvements or emerging trends in the security posture of your IT environment.

10. Export Reports for Documentation:

If needed, export the report in a suitable format (e.g., PDF) for documentation and sharing with stakeholders. Documentation is essential for audit purposes, compliance reporting, and communication with management and IT teams.

11. Collaborate with Teams:

Share the report findings with relevant teams, including system administrators, IT personnel, and security teams. Collaboration ensures that remediation efforts are coordinated and aligned with organizational priorities.

12. Develop Remediation Plan:

Based on the analysis, develop a remediation plan that outlines the steps to address identified vulnerabilities. Prioritize remediation efforts according to severity levels and potential impact on business operations.

13. Iterate and Improve:

Use the insights gained from the report analysis to iterate and improve your vulnerability management process. Adjust scanning configurations, refine remediation strategies, and incorporate lessons learned into future assessments.

Analyzing OpenVAS reports is a dynamic process that involves understanding the security landscape of your organization, prioritizing remediation efforts, and collaborating with relevant teams. By regularly reviewing and acting upon the findings, you contribute to a proactive and effective approach to vulnerability management, strengthening the overall security posture of your IT infrastructure.

6.2 Prioritizing Identified Vulnerabilities

Effectively prioritizing identified vulnerabilities is crucial for organizations to focus their resources on addressing the most critical security risks first. OpenVAS reports provide valuable information on vulnerabilities, including their severity levels. Here's a guide on how to prioritize identified vulnerabilities in OpenVAS reports:

1. Understand Severity Levels:

OpenVAS categorizes vulnerabilities into severity levels, such as critical, high, medium, and low. Understand the significance of each level:

- **Critical**: Represents vulnerabilities that pose an immediate and severe threat to the security of the system. Immediate attention and remediation are often required.
- **High**: Indicates significant vulnerabilities that should be addressed promptly to reduce the risk of exploitation.
- **Medium**: Represents moderate-level vulnerabilities that require attention but may not pose an immediate threat.
- **Low**: Denotes lower-risk vulnerabilities that can be addressed based on organizational priorities.

2. Focus on Critical and High-Severity Vulnerabilities:

Prioritize the remediation of critical and high-severity vulnerabilities. These vulnerabilities have the potential to cause significant harm and are more likely to be targeted by attackers. Immediate attention should be given to addressing these issues.

3. Consider the Affected Assets:

Take into account the assets affected by vulnerabilities. Critical and high-severity vulnerabilities on critical assets, such as servers hosting sensitive data, should be addressed with higher priority than similar vulnerabilities on less critical systems.

4. Evaluate Potential Impact:

Assess the potential impact of each vulnerability on business operations, data confidentiality, and system integrity. Consider the consequences of a successful exploitation and prioritize vulnerabilities that could have the most detrimental effects.

5. Look for Actively Exploited Vulnerabilities:

Identify vulnerabilities that are actively exploited in the wild. OpenVAS may provide information on whether a vulnerability is known to be exploited. Addressing such vulnerabilities promptly is essential to prevent exploitation.

6. Consider Vulnerability Chains:

Evaluate vulnerabilities in the context of potential vulnerability chains. Some vulnerabilities, when combined, may pose a greater risk than when assessed individually. Consider the cumulative impact of multiple vulnerabilities.

7. Assess Attack Vectors:

Understand the likely attack vectors associated with each vulnerability. Consider vulnerabilities that can be exploited remotely or without authentication as higher priorities, as they may be more accessible to attackers.

8. Review Industry Threat Intelligence:

Stay informed about industry threat intelligence to identify emerging threats and vulnerabilities. Consider prioritizing vulnerabilities that align with known attack trends and prevalent security risks.

9. Collaborate with Teams:

Collaborate with system administrators, IT teams, and security personnel to gather additional insights. Teams can provide context about the criticality of assets, potential business impact, and feasibility of remediation.

10. Develop a Remediation Plan:

Based on the prioritization, develop a remediation plan that outlines the steps to address identified vulnerabilities. Clearly communicate the plan to relevant stakeholders and ensure coordination among teams.

11. Iterate and Update:

Regularly iterate on the prioritization process based on feedback, emerging threats, and changes in the organizational landscape. Update the prioritization criteria to reflect evolving security requirements.

Prioritizing identified vulnerabilities is a strategic process that involves understanding the risk landscape, considering severity levels, and aligning remediation efforts with organizational priorities. By focusing on critical and high-severity vulnerabilities that pose the greatest risk, organizations can proactively enhance their security posture and reduce the likelihood of successful cyberattacks. Regular reviews and updates to the prioritization strategy contribute to an adaptive and effective vulnerability management approach.

6.3 Generating Actionable Insights

Generating actionable insights from OpenVAS reports is essential for organizations to make informed decisions, prioritize remediation efforts, and enhance their overall cybersecurity posture. Here's a guide on how to transform OpenVAS reports into actionable insights:

1. Understand Business Context:

Begin by understanding the business context and priorities. Align the interpretation of vulnerabilities with the organization's critical assets, business processes, and regulatory requirements. Consider the potential impact of vulnerabilities on business operations.

2. Prioritize High-Impact Vulnerabilities:

Focus on high-impact vulnerabilities that could have severe consequences if exploited. Prioritize vulnerabilities based on their potential impact on confidentiality, integrity, and availability of systems and data.

3. Segment Assets by Criticality:

Segment assets based on criticality to the organization. Classify systems and data according to their importance to business operations. Prioritize remediation efforts on critical assets to minimize the impact of potential security breaches.

4. Consider Attack Vectors:

Analyze vulnerabilities in the context of likely attack vectors. Prioritize vulnerabilities that can be exploited remotely, without authentication, or through commonly used attack methods. Understanding potential attack scenarios helps in focusing mitigation efforts.

5. Review False Positives and Negatives:

Examine the report for false positives and false negatives. Addressing false positives ensures that resources are not wasted on non-existent issues, while identifying false negatives helps uncover overlooked vulnerabilities that may require attention.

6. Engage with Stakeholders:

Collaborate with relevant stakeholders, including system administrators, IT teams, and security professionals. Gain additional insights into the operational context, system configurations, and feasibility of implementing remediation measures.

7. Develop Remediation Strategies:

Develop clear and actionable remediation strategies for identified vulnerabilities. Outline specific steps to address each vulnerability, considering the technical aspects, resource requirements, and potential impacts on operations.

8. Implement Patch Management:

Integrate identified vulnerabilities into the organization's patch management process. Prioritize and schedule patches based on severity levels and criticality. Ensure that patches are tested and deployed in a timely manner to mitigate vulnerabilities.

9. Automate Remediation Tasks:

Where possible, automate remediation tasks to enhance efficiency. Use automation tools to apply patches, configure security settings, or deploy mitigations. Automation helps streamline the remediation process and reduces manual effort.

10. Monitor Progress and Compliance:

Regularly monitor the progress of remediation efforts. Track the implementation of patches, configuration changes, or other security measures. Ensure compliance with organizational policies and regulatory requirements throughout the remediation process.

11. Generate Trend Analysis:

Aggregate and analyze data from multiple OpenVAS reports to identify trends over time. Track improvements in vulnerability management, identify recurring issues, and assess the overall effectiveness of security measures.

12. Document Lessons Learned:

Document lessons learned from each remediation cycle. Capture insights into the effectiveness of mitigation strategies, challenges encountered, and areas for improvement. Use this information to refine future vulnerability management processes.

13. Iterate and Improve:

Continuously iterate and improve the vulnerability management process based on feedback, evolving threats, and changes in the organization. Regularly update strategies, tools, and methodologies to stay ahead of emerging cybersecurity challenges.

Generating actionable insights from OpenVAS reports requires a holistic approach that considers business context, prioritization, collaboration, and continuous improvement. By transforming vulnerability assessments into practical and strategic measures, organizations can enhance their ability to mitigate risks, respond to emerging threats, and maintain a resilient security posture. Regular reviews, collaboration, and adaptive strategies contribute to an effective and sustainable vulnerability management program.

7. Automating Vulnerability Assessments

In the dynamic landscape of cybersecurity, where threats evolve at a relentless pace, the ability to respond swiftly and proactively is paramount. Chapter 7 ushers us into the realm of automation—an indispensable facet of modern cybersecurity strategy. Here, we explore how OpenVAS can be harnessed to automate vulnerability assessments, providing a continuous, vigilant shield against potential threats.

Setting Up Automated Scans: A Continuous Watchman

The journey begins with the first subchapter, delving into the process of setting up automated scans. Automation is not merely a convenience; it's a continuous watchman, tirelessly patrolling your digital landscape. We unravel the intricacies of scheduling scans, defining recurring assessments, and configuring OpenVAS to operate as an autonomous guardian against emerging vulnerabilities.

Scheduling Regular Assessments: The Rhythm of Security

In the second subchapter, we dive into the importance of scheduling regular assessments. Just as a routine health check ensures the vitality of the human body, regular vulnerability assessments maintain the health of your digital infrastructure. We guide you through the nuances of establishing assessment rhythms, ensuring that your automated scans align with the evolving nature of your systems and networks.

Integration with Task Automation Tools: Streamlining Defenses

The final subchapter explores the integration of OpenVAS with task automation tools. As cybersecurity professionals, your toolbox extends beyond a single application. Here, we provide insights into seamlessly integrating OpenVAS into broader security workflows, creating a harmonious symphony of automated defenses that respond cohesively to potential threats.

As Chapter 7 unfolds, you will not only grasp the mechanics of automating vulnerability assessments with OpenVAS but also appreciate the strategic advantages of continuous vigilance. Join us in this exploration of automation, where efficiency and responsiveness become the hallmarks of a resilient cybersecurity posture.

7.1 Setting Up Automated Scans

Automating vulnerability scans in OpenVAS streamlines the process of regularly assessing your IT infrastructure's security posture. Automated scans ensure that your organization stays proactive in identifying and addressing potential vulnerabilities. Here's a guide on setting up automated scans in OpenVAS:

1. Access the Greenbone Security Assistant (GSA):

Open your web browser and log in to the Greenbone Security Assistant, the web-based interface for OpenVAS. Navigate to the "Scans" section, where you can manage and configure vulnerability scans.

2. Create a New Scan Configuration:

If you haven't already, create a new scan configuration specifically tailored for automated scans. Click on the "Create" or "New" button to initiate the creation of a scan configuration.

3. Configure General Scan Settings:

Define general settings for the automated scan configuration. This includes providing a descriptive name, selecting the target systems or IP ranges to scan, and specifying other parameters like scan speed and timing.

4. Specify Scan Targets:

Clearly define the scope of the automated scan by specifying the target systems or networks. You can enter individual IP addresses, define IP ranges, or use predefined target groups. Ensure that the targets accurately represent the systems you want to assess.

5. Choose Scan Configurations:

Select the appropriate scan configurations for the automated scan. OpenVAS provides predefined configurations such as "Full and Fast," "Full and Fast Ultimate," and others. Choose a configuration that aligns with your organization's scanning goals.

6. Configure Authentication (If Applicable):

If your automated scans require authentication, configure the necessary authentication settings. Provide usernames, passwords, or other credentials required to access the target systems. Authenticated scans provide deeper insights into system security.

7. Schedule the Automated Scan:

Schedule the automated scan for regular intervals to ensure continuous vulnerability assessment. Specify the frequency (daily, weekly, monthly) and the time at which the scan should occur. Scheduled scans help maintain an up-to-date security posture.

8. Set Recurrence and Duration:

Specify how often the automated scan should recur and the duration it should run. Consider factors such as network load, system availability, and resource constraints when setting recurrence and duration parameters.

9. Configure Reporting Options:

Define the reporting options for the automated scan. Specify whether you want detailed reports, summary reports, or both. Configure the format in which reports should be generated, such as PDF or XML.

10. Enable Email Notifications (Optional):

If your organization requires immediate notification of scan results, enable email notifications. Configure the email settings, including recipients, subject, and content. Email notifications keep relevant stakeholders informed about the scan outcomes.

11. Save the Automated Scan Configuration:

Once you've configured all the settings for the automated scan, save the configuration. This ensures that the scan parameters are stored and can be easily reused for future automated scans.

12. Initiate the Automated Scan:

Manually initiate the automated scan to verify that the configuration works as expected. Confirm that the scan starts at the scheduled time, targets the specified systems, and generates the desired reports.

13. Monitor and Review Results:

Regularly monitor the results of automated scans through the OpenVAS interface. Review scan reports, identify newly discovered vulnerabilities, and prioritize remediation efforts based on severity levels.

14. Adjust Settings as Needed:

Periodically review and adjust the automated scan configuration based on organizational changes, system updates, or evolving security requirements. Ensure that the scan parameters remain aligned with the current IT landscape.

Setting up automated scans in OpenVAS is a proactive measure to continuously assess and enhance the security of your IT infrastructure. By configuring automated scans with careful consideration of targets, scheduling, and reporting, organizations can establish a robust vulnerability management process that adapts to changing security needs. Regularly reviewing and adjusting automated scan configurations ensures that the vulnerability assessment remains effective and aligned with organizational priorities.

7.2 Scheduling Regular Assessments

Scheduling regular assessments in OpenVAS is a fundamental practice for maintaining an up-to-date understanding of your IT infrastructure's security posture. Regular scans help identify new vulnerabilities, track changes in the network, and ensure ongoing compliance with security policies. Here's a guide on how to schedule regular assessments in OpenVAS:

1. Access the Greenbone Security Assistant (GSA):

Open your web browser and log in to the Greenbone Security Assistant, the web-based interface for OpenVAS. Navigate to the "Scans" section, where you can manage and schedule vulnerability assessments.

2. Create or Select a Scan Configuration:

If you already have a dedicated scan configuration for regular assessments, select it. Otherwise, create a new scan configuration specifically tailored for recurring scans. Click on the "Create" or "New" button to initiate the configuration process.

3. Configure General Scan Settings:

Define general settings for the scan configuration. Provide a descriptive name for the scan, select the target systems or IP ranges to assess, and specify parameters such as scan speed and timing. Ensure that the configuration aligns with your organization's scanning goals.

4. Specify Scan Targets:

Clearly define the scope of the scan by specifying the target systems or networks. You can use IP addresses, IP ranges, or predefined target groups. Ensure that the targets accurately represent the systems you want to assess during each recurring scan.

5. Choose Scan Configurations:

Select the appropriate scan configurations for the regular assessments. Predefined configurations such as "Full and Fast," "Full and Fast Ultimate," and others are available. Choose a configuration that balances thoroughness and resource efficiency based on your scanning goals.

6. Configure Authentication (If Applicable):

If your regular assessments require authentication, configure the necessary settings. Provide usernames, passwords, or other credentials required to access the target systems. Authenticated scans provide more comprehensive insights into system security.

7. Schedule the Recurring Assessment:

In the configuration settings, set up the recurring schedule for the assessment. Specify the frequency (daily, weekly, monthly) and the time at which the scan should occur. Scheduled assessments ensure that vulnerability assessments are conducted consistently over time.

8. Set Recurrence and Duration:

Specify how often the recurring assessments should recur and the duration they should run. Consider factors such as network load, system availability, and resource constraints when setting recurrence and duration parameters.

9. Configure Reporting Options:

Define the reporting options for the regular assessments. Specify whether you want detailed reports, summary reports, or both. Configure the format in which reports should be generated, such as PDF or XML.

10. Enable Email Notifications (Optional):

If your organization requires immediate notification of assessment results, enable email notifications. Configure the email settings, including recipients, subject, and content. Email notifications keep relevant stakeholders informed about the assessment outcomes.

11. Save the Configuration:

Once you've configured all the settings for the recurring assessment, save the configuration. This ensures that the parameters are stored and can be easily reused for future scheduled assessments.

12. Initiate the First Scheduled Assessment:

Manually initiate the first scheduled assessment to confirm that the configuration works as expected. Verify that the assessment starts at the scheduled time, targets the specified systems, and generates the desired reports.

13. Monitor and Review Results:

Regularly monitor the results of the scheduled assessments through the OpenVAS interface. Review scan reports, identify newly discovered vulnerabilities, and prioritize remediation efforts based on severity levels.

14. Adjust Settings as Needed:

Periodically review and adjust the scheduled assessment configuration based on organizational changes, system updates, or evolving security requirements. Ensure that the assessment parameters remain aligned with the current IT landscape.

Scheduling regular assessments in OpenVAS is a proactive approach to maintaining a vigilant security posture. By configuring recurring scans with careful consideration of targets, scheduling, and reporting, organizations can establish a continuous vulnerability management process that adapts to changing security needs. Regularly reviewing and adjusting scheduled assessment configurations ensures that the vulnerability assessments remain effective and aligned with organizational priorities.

7.3 Integration with Task Automation Tools

Integrating OpenVAS with task automation tools enhances the efficiency and effectiveness of vulnerability management processes. Automation streamlines repetitive tasks, accelerates response times, and ensures a more proactive approach to security. Here's a guide on integrating OpenVAS with task automation tools:

1. Select a Task Automation Tool:

Choose a task automation tool that aligns with your organization's preferences and existing infrastructure. Popular options include Ansible, Puppet, Chef, or custom scripting using languages like Python or Bash.

2. Understand OpenVAS APIs:

Familiarize yourself with OpenVAS APIs (Application Programming Interfaces). OpenVAS provides APIs that allow external tools to interact with the system. Understanding the APIs is essential for seamless integration with automation tools.

3. Generate API Key in OpenVAS:

In the Greenbone Security Assistant (GSA), generate an API key that will be used by the task automation tool to authenticate and communicate with OpenVAS. This key serves as a secure method for accessing OpenVAS resources.

4. Configure Task Automation Tool:

In your chosen task automation tool, configure the necessary settings to establish a connection with OpenVAS. This includes providing the OpenVAS server address, port, and the API key generated in the previous step.

5. Automate Scan Launch and Scheduling:

Utilize the task automation tool to automate the launch and scheduling of vulnerability scans. This involves creating scripts or playbooks that trigger OpenVAS scans based on predefined configurations. Automated scheduling ensures regular assessments without manual intervention.

6. Integrate Scan Results Analysis:

Automate the analysis of scan results using the task automation tool. Develop scripts or playbooks that parse and interpret OpenVAS reports, extracting relevant information about identified vulnerabilities, their severity, and affected hosts.

7. Automate Remediation Tasks:

Implement automation for remediation tasks based on scan results. Develop scripts or playbooks that automatically apply patches, update configurations, or initiate other remediation measures. This accelerates the response to identified vulnerabilities.

8. Implement Custom Workflows:

Create custom workflows that integrate OpenVAS into your organization's broader security processes. Automation tools can facilitate the coordination of actions across different security solutions, creating a more cohesive and responsive security ecosystem.

9. Enable Notification and Reporting:

Configure the task automation tool to send notifications based on scan results. Automated notifications can alert relevant stakeholders about critical vulnerabilities, enabling prompt response and remediation.

10. Regularly Update Automation Scripts:

Stay proactive by regularly updating and refining your automation scripts or playbooks. As OpenVAS evolves or organizational requirements change, ensure that your automation tools are synchronized and optimized for the latest capabilities.

11. Implement Version Control:

Use version control systems (e.g., Git) to manage and track changes in your automation scripts or playbooks. Version control ensures accountability, facilitates collaboration, and enables rollbacks in case of issues.

12. Monitor Automation Performance:

Implement monitoring and logging mechanisms to track the performance of your automation workflows. Monitor for errors, delays, or other issues to promptly address any anomalies and ensure the reliability of automated processes.

13. Collaborate with Security Teams:

Collaborate with your organization's security teams to align automation efforts with overall security strategies. Ensure that automated processes adhere to security policies, compliance requirements, and best practices.

14. Document and Share Knowledge:

Document your automation workflows comprehensively and share knowledge within the team. Clear documentation facilitates knowledge transfer, troubleshooting, and the ongoing improvement of automation processes.

Integration with task automation tools empowers organizations to orchestrate and streamline vulnerability management activities in OpenVAS. By automating scans, analysis, and remediation tasks, organizations can achieve a more proactive and responsive security posture. Regularly updating and optimizing automation workflows ensures that the integration remains effective in addressing evolving security challenges.

8. Advanced Configuration and Customization

As we ascend further into the echelons of OpenVAS mastery, Chapter 8 unfurls the realm of advanced configuration and customization. Here, we transcend the basics, delving into the nuanced art of fine-tuning scan policies, customizing vulnerability checks, and leveraging bespoke scripts and plugins. In this chapter, OpenVAS transforms from a tool into a finely tuned instrument, calibrated precisely to the unique contours of your cybersecurity landscape.

Fine-Tuning Scan Policies: Precision in Action

The initial subchapter plunges into the intricacies of fine-tuning scan policies. Like a maestro orchestrating a symphony, you will learn to refine the parameters of your vulnerability scans, ensuring that they resonate harmoniously with the specific security needs of your organization. From tweaking performance settings to customizing scan configurations, this section empowers you to conduct assessments with surgical precision.

Customizing Vulnerability Checks: Tailoring Your Defense

With the foundation of fine-tuned scans in place, the journey progresses to the second subchapter, where we explore the art of customizing vulnerability checks. Every organization has unique vulnerabilities, and OpenVAS allows you to craft bespoke checks that align with your specific risk landscape. Unleash the power of customization to identify vulnerabilities that might escape generic assessments, transforming OpenVAS into a customized guardian for your digital assets.

Using Custom Scripts and Plugins: Elevating Your Arsenal

The final subchapter elevates your cybersecurity arsenal by delving into the utilization of custom scripts and plugins within OpenVAS. Here, you will discover how to extend the functionality of OpenVAS through the integration of tailor-made scripts and plugins. Elevating your capabilities, these custom additions empower you to address specialized vulnerabilities and enhance the overall effectiveness of your vulnerability assessments.

As Chapter 8 unfolds, you will not only traverse the advanced terrain of OpenVAS but also acquire the skills needed to sculpt this powerful tool into a bespoke instrument of cybersecurity defense. Join us in this exploration of precision, where fine-tuning and customization become your allies in the relentless pursuit of a secure digital landscape.

8.1 Fine-Tuning Scan Policies

Fine-tuning scan policies in OpenVAS is essential to ensure that vulnerability assessments are tailored to the specific requirements and nuances of your organization's IT environment. Customizing scan policies helps optimize the accuracy and relevance of scan results. Here's a guide on fine-tuning scan policies in OpenVAS:

1. Access the Greenbone Security Assistant (GSA):

Open your web browser and log in to the Greenbone Security Assistant, the web-based interface for OpenVAS. Navigate to the "Configuration" or "Scan Configs" section where you can manage and fine-tune scan policies.

2. Review Default Scan Configurations:

Understand the default scan configurations provided by OpenVAS, such as "Full and Fast," "Full and Fast Ultimate," and others. These configurations serve as starting points and can be customized based on your organization's specific needs.

3. Create a New Scan Configuration:

If you need to create a new scan policy or fine-tune an existing one, click on the "Create" or "New" button to initiate the creation of a scan configuration.

4. Specify Target Systems:

Define the target systems or networks for the scan. Specify IP addresses, IP ranges, or use predefined target groups. Ensure that the targets accurately represent the systems you want to assess and consider any segmentation within your network.

5. Adjust Scan Speed:

Fine-tune the scan speed based on the network environment and resource availability. Consider the impact of scanning on network performance and adjust the speed accordingly. Options often include "Slow," "Normal," and "Fast."

6. Configure Port Scanning Options:

Customize port scanning options based on your organization's requirements. You can configure settings such as port ranges, TCP or UDP scanning, and the use of specific port scanning algorithms.

7. Enable/Disable Vulnerability Checks:

Select specific vulnerability checks to include or exclude based on your organization's priorities. Enabling or disabling checks allows you to focus on specific types of vulnerabilities relevant to your IT environment.

8. Adjust Host Discovery Settings:

Fine-tune host discovery settings to optimize the identification of active hosts. Configure options such as host timeouts, host grouping, and discovery of hosts through services.

9. Customize Safe Checks:

Safe checks are designed to minimize the impact of the scan on target systems. Customize safe check settings based on the sensitivity of your systems. These checks are less likely to cause disruptions but may provide fewer details.

10. Configure Credentials (If Applicable):

If authenticated scans are part of your vulnerability management strategy, configure credentials for accessing target systems. Authenticated scans provide more comprehensive insights into the security posture of systems.

11. Fine-Tune Scan Timing:

Adjust the timing of the scan to minimize the impact on network and system performance. Schedule scans during periods of lower activity to reduce the likelihood of disruptions to critical operations.

12. Define Scan Exclusions:

Specify any exclusions or exceptions for the scan. Exclude certain IP addresses, hosts, or ranges that should not be included in the vulnerability assessment. This is particularly relevant for special-purpose or critical systems.

13. Review Compliance Checks:

If compliance checks are part of your scan policy, review and customize them based on your organization's regulatory requirements and security policies. Compliance checks help ensure that systems adhere to specific standards.

14. Save and Test the Scan Policy:

Once you've fine-tuned the scan policy, save the configuration, and conduct test scans. Testing helps ensure that the policy works as intended and provides the desired results. Validate that the scans align with your security goals.

15. Iterate and Update:

Regularly iterate on your scan policies based on feedback, changes in the IT environment, and evolving security requirements. Keep scan policies up to date to address emerging threats and vulnerabilities.

Fine-tuning scan policies in OpenVAS is a critical aspect of effective vulnerability management. By customizing scan configurations to align with your organization's specific needs, you can enhance the accuracy and relevance of vulnerability assessments. Regularly reviewing and updating scan policies ensures that your vulnerability management strategy remains adaptive and effective in the ever-changing landscape of cybersecurity.

8.2 Customizing Vulnerability Checks

Customizing vulnerability checks in OpenVAS allows organizations to tailor their vulnerability assessments to specific requirements, focusing on the nuances of their IT environment. By fine-tuning and customizing vulnerability checks, you can optimize the accuracy and relevance of scan results. Here's a guide on customizing vulnerability checks in OpenVAS:

1. Access the Greenbone Security Assistant (GSA):

Open your web browser and log in to the Greenbone Security Assistant, the web-based interface for OpenVAS. Navigate to the "Configuration" or "Vulnerability Tests" section where you can manage and customize vulnerability checks.

2. Understand Default Vulnerability Checks:

Gain an understanding of the default vulnerability checks provided by OpenVAS. These checks cover a wide range of security issues and serve as the foundation for your vulnerability assessments.

3. Review Categories and Families:

Vulnerability checks are organized into categories and families. Familiarize yourself with these classifications to better navigate and customize checks based on your organization's priorities.

4. Identify Relevant Checks:

Review the list of vulnerability checks and identify those most relevant to your IT environment. Prioritize checks based on the technologies, applications, and systems used within your organization.

5. Create Custom Vulnerability Tests:

If there are specific checks you need that are not covered by default, create custom vulnerability tests. Define the parameters, conditions, and criteria for these tests to effectively assess your unique set of security concerns.

6. Modify Existing Checks:

Customize existing vulnerability checks to better suit your organization's requirements. Adjust parameters, thresholds, or conditions to align checks with your understanding of what constitutes a security risk in your environment.

7. Adjust Severity Levels:

Fine-tune the severity levels assigned to vulnerability checks based on your organization's risk tolerance and prioritization. Customize severity levels to ensure that the impact and urgency of identified vulnerabilities align with your security policies.

8. Include or Exclude Checks:

Customize the list of vulnerability checks included in your scans. Include checks that are critical to your organization and exclude those that may not be relevant or are known false positives.

9. Configure Check Dependencies:

Define dependencies between vulnerability checks if certain checks are interrelated. Configuring dependencies ensures that the assessment considers the potential chain of vulnerabilities that could be exploited.

10. Review and Apply Test Scripts:

If your organization utilizes custom test scripts or plugins, review and apply them to enhance the coverage of your vulnerability assessments. Ensure that the scripts align with your organization's security objectives.

11. Test Customized Checks:

Before deploying customized vulnerability checks in production scans, thoroughly test them in a controlled environment. Testing helps identify any issues, false positives, or false negatives and ensures the reliability of the customized checks.

12. Document Customizations:

Document all customizations made to vulnerability checks, including the rationale behind each modification. Documentation is crucial for knowledge transfer, audit purposes, and maintaining an understanding of the organization's security posture.

13. Collaborate with Security Teams:

Collaborate with your organization's security teams to gather insights into the relevance and impact of specific vulnerability checks. Regular communication ensures that customizations align with the overall security strategy.

14. Regularly Update Customizations:

Vulnerability landscapes and IT environments evolve. Regularly update and refine your custom vulnerability checks to adapt to emerging threats, technological changes, and shifts in organizational priorities.

15. Iterate and Improve:

Continuously iterate on your customization process based on feedback, lessons learned, and changes in the security landscape. Implement improvements to ensure that your vulnerability checks remain effective and aligned with organizational goals.

Customizing vulnerability checks in OpenVAS is a strategic approach to enhancing the precision and relevance of your vulnerability assessments. By tailoring checks to the specific needs of your organization, you can focus on the security issues that matter most and strengthen your overall cybersecurity posture. Regular updates and collaboration with security teams contribute to an adaptive and effective vulnerability management strategy.

8.3 Leveraging Custom Scripts and Plugins

Leveraging custom scripts and plugins in OpenVAS enhances the capability of vulnerability assessments by allowing organizations to address specific security concerns, technologies, or scenarios unique to their IT environment. Custom scripts and plugins provide flexibility and depth in assessing vulnerabilities. Here's a guide on how to leverage custom scripts and plugins in OpenVAS:

1. Access the Greenbone Security Assistant (GSA):

Open your web browser and log in to the Greenbone Security Assistant, the web-based interface for OpenVAS. Navigate to the "Configuration" or "Plugins" section where you can manage and leverage custom scripts and plugins.

2. Understand OpenVAS Scripting and NASL:

OpenVAS uses the Nessus Attack Scripting Language (NASL) for vulnerability checks. Familiarize yourself with NASL to understand how to create and utilize custom scripts and plugins.

3. Identify Specific Security Concerns:

Identify specific security concerns or scenarios within your organization that are not adequately covered by default vulnerability checks. These could include proprietary applications, specialized technologies, or industry-specific requirements.

4. Create Custom NASL Scripts:

Develop custom NASL scripts to address the identified security concerns. NASL scripts are written to define how OpenVAS should perform vulnerability checks for specific issues. Ensure that your scripts adhere to NASL syntax and best practices.

5. Test Custom Scripts:

Thoroughly test your custom NASL scripts in a controlled environment before deploying them in production scans. Testing helps identify any issues, false positives, or false negatives and ensures the reliability of the custom scripts.

6. Implement Script Dependency Management:

If your organization utilizes multiple custom scripts, implement script dependency management. Define dependencies between scripts to ensure that assessments consider the potential chain of vulnerabilities that could be exploited.

7. Integrate External Plugins:

Explore the option of integrating external plugins or third-party scripts that are relevant to your organization's security objectives. Ensure that these plugins are compatible with the version of OpenVAS you are using.

8. Review Plugin Documentation:

If you are incorporating external plugins, review the accompanying documentation thoroughly. Understand how the plugins work, their scope, and any configuration parameters that may be required for effective use.

9. Configure Plugin Execution:

Configure the execution of custom scripts and plugins within the OpenVAS environment. Specify parameters, dependencies, and any other settings necessary for the proper functioning of the custom scripts and plugins.

10. Document Customizations:

Document all custom scripts and plugins, including the purpose, functionality, and any dependencies. Documentation is crucial for knowledge transfer, audit purposes, and maintaining an understanding of the organization's security posture.

11. Collaborate with Security Teams:

Collaborate with your organization's security teams to gather insights into the relevance and impact of specific custom scripts and plugins. Regular communication ensures that customizations align with the overall security strategy.

12. Regularly Update Custom Scripts:

As the IT environment evolves, regularly update and refine your custom scripts and plugins to adapt to emerging threats, technological changes, and shifts in organizational priorities.

13. Iterate and Improve:

Continuously iterate on your custom scripting and plugin management process based on feedback, lessons learned, and changes in the security landscape. Implement improvements to ensure that your customizations remain effective and aligned with organizational goals.

Leveraging custom scripts and plugins in OpenVAS provides organizations with the flexibility to address specific security concerns and tailor vulnerability assessments to their unique IT environment. By creating and managing custom NASL scripts and integrating external plugins, organizations can enhance the depth and precision of their vulnerability management strategy. Regular updates and collaboration with security teams contribute to an adaptive and effective approach to addressing evolving security challenges.

9. OpenVAS Best Practices

In the ever-evolving landscape of cybersecurity, where threats morph and digital landscapes transform, the significance of adhering to best practices cannot be overstated. Chapter 9 serves as your guide to OpenVAS best practices—an essential compass that navigates you through the intricacies of effective vulnerability assessment, ensuring that your Open Vulnerability Assessment System becomes a stalwart guardian rather than a mere tool.

Effective Use Guidelines: Maximizing Impact

The journey begins with the exploration of effective use guidelines. Beyond the technicalities, we delve into the strategic principles that enhance the impact of your vulnerability assessments. From optimal scan configurations to strategic scheduling, this subchapter equips you with guidelines that transcend routine use, elevating OpenVAS to a proactive cybersecurity asset.

Security Considerations and Precautions: Fortifying Defenses

In the second subchapter, we turn our attention to the critical realm of security considerations and precautions. As you harness the power of OpenVAS, it becomes imperative to fortify your defenses against potential pitfalls and vulnerabilities introduced during the assessment process. Here, we guide you through security best practices, ensuring that your use of OpenVAS aligns seamlessly with the overarching goal of safeguarding your digital domain.

Compliance and Regulatory Implications: Navigating the Landscape

The final subchapter unfolds the complex terrain of compliance and regulatory implications. In an era where data protection laws and industry standards are paramount, understanding how OpenVAS aligns with these regulations is not a choice but a necessity. We explore best practices for ensuring compliance, providing you with the insights needed to navigate the intricate landscape of cybersecurity regulations confidently.

As Chapter 9 unfurls, you will not only absorb the technical best practices for OpenVAS but also internalize the strategic principles that elevate your vulnerability assessments to a level of excellence. Join us in this exploration of best practices, where each guideline is a step closer to a cybersecurity posture that is both effective and resilient.

9.1 Effective Use Guidelines

To maximize the benefits of OpenVAS in your cybersecurity vulnerability assessment efforts, it's crucial to follow effective use guidelines. These guidelines help ensure that OpenVAS is utilized optimally and aligns with your organization's security goals. Here's a comprehensive set of guidelines for the effective use of OpenVAS:

1. Define Clear Objectives:

Clearly define the objectives of your vulnerability assessments using OpenVAS. Understand what you aim to achieve, whether it's regulatory compliance, risk reduction, or proactive threat mitigation.

2. Regularly Update OpenVAS:

Keep your OpenVAS installation up to date with the latest security feeds, vulnerability checks, and software updates. Regular updates ensure that you benefit from the latest threat intelligence and detection capabilities.

3. Establish a Scanning Schedule:

Create a regular scanning schedule to ensure ongoing monitoring of your IT infrastructure. Scheduled scans help identify and address vulnerabilities promptly and maintain a proactive security stance.

4. Customize Scan Configurations:

Tailor scan configurations to suit your organization's needs. Fine-tune parameters such as scan speed, target systems, and vulnerability check selection to optimize scan accuracy and relevance.

5. Leverage Authentication for Deeper Insights:

Implement authenticated scans whenever possible to gain deeper insights into the security posture of your systems. Authenticated scans provide more accurate and comprehensive vulnerability assessments.

6. Prioritize High-Impact Vulnerabilities:

Focus on addressing high-impact vulnerabilities first. Prioritize remediation efforts based on the severity and potential impact of vulnerabilities on your organization's assets and operations.

7. Regularly Review and Update Policies:

Periodically review and update your scan policies to adapt to changes in your IT environment, emerging threats, and evolving security requirements. Ensure that scan policies remain aligned with organizational goals.

8. Implement Automated Scans:

Utilize automated scans to streamline vulnerability assessments and ensure consistent coverage. Automate repetitive tasks such as scan launches, report generation, and result analysis to save time and resources.

9. Integrate with Task Automation Tools:

Integrate OpenVAS with task automation tools to orchestrate and automate vulnerability management processes. Automation enhances efficiency and responsiveness in addressing security vulnerabilities.

10. Collaborate with Security Teams:

Maintain open communication with your organization's security teams. Collaborate on vulnerability management strategies, share insights, and align OpenVAS activities with broader security initiatives.

11. Regularly Monitor and Analyze Reports:

Regularly monitor and analyze OpenVAS scan reports. Identify trends, track improvements, and use the insights gained to make informed decisions regarding vulnerability remediation.

12. Implement a Patch Management Process:

Integrate OpenVAS findings into a robust patch management process. Ensure that patches are applied in a timely manner, especially for critical vulnerabilities, to mitigate potential security risks.

13. Document and Report Findings:

Document all scan findings, remediation efforts, and outcomes. Generate comprehensive reports that can be shared with relevant stakeholders, auditors, and management to demonstrate the organization's commitment to cybersecurity.

14. Conduct Regular Training for Users:

Educate and train users within your organization on the importance of cybersecurity hygiene and the role they play in maintaining a secure IT environment. Awareness contributes to a collective effort in reducing vulnerabilities.

15. Adhere to Compliance Requirements:

Ensure that your vulnerability assessments align with regulatory compliance requirements relevant to your industry. Adhering to compliance standards helps maintain a secure and legally compliant IT infrastructure.

16. Establish Incident Response Procedures:

Have well-defined incident response procedures in place. Prepare for the possibility of a security incident and establish protocols for quickly responding to and mitigating the impact of a security breach.

17. Regularly Backup OpenVAS Configurations:

Back up your OpenVAS configurations regularly to safeguard critical settings, policies, and scan results. A comprehensive backup strategy ensures that you can quickly recover from unexpected issues.

18. Engage in Community Forums:

Participate in OpenVAS community forums to stay informed about updates, best practices, and common challenges. Engaging with the community provides valuable insights and support for effective OpenVAS usage.

Following these effective use guidelines for OpenVAS empowers your organization to conduct robust and proactive vulnerability assessments. By aligning OpenVAS activities with organizational goals, staying updated, and implementing best practices, you can enhance your cybersecurity posture and reduce the risk of potential security threats. Regular evaluation and improvement of your OpenVAS deployment contribute to a resilient and secure IT infrastructure.

9.2 Security Considerations and Precautions

While OpenVAS is a powerful tool for cybersecurity vulnerability assessments, it's important to implement security considerations and precautions to ensure the integrity, confidentiality, and availability of your IT infrastructure. Here are essential security considerations and precautions for using OpenVAS:

1. Secure Access Control:

Implement strict access controls for OpenVAS components, especially the Greenbone Security Assistant (GSA) and the underlying OpenVAS Manager. Restrict access to authorized personnel and enforce strong authentication mechanisms.

2. Use HTTPS for Web Interface:

Configure the Greenbone Security Assistant (GSA) to use HTTPS for secure communication. Encrypting web traffic helps protect sensitive information, such as login credentials and scan results, from eavesdropping and interception.

3. Regularly Update and Patch:

Stay vigilant about updating OpenVAS components and dependencies regularly. Apply patches and updates promptly to address security vulnerabilities and benefit from the latest features and security enhancements.

4. Secure Communication Channels:

Ensure that communication channels between OpenVAS components, including the scanner, manager, and web interface, are secured. Implement encryption protocols such as TLS to protect data in transit.

5. Limit Network Exposure:

Minimize the exposure of OpenVAS to the external network. Place OpenVAS components behind firewalls and only expose necessary ports. Restrict external access to critical OpenVAS infrastructure components.

6. Strong Password Policies:

Enforce strong password policies for user accounts associated with OpenVAS. Require complex passwords, and regularly update and rotate passwords to enhance authentication security.

7. Monitoring and Logging:

Implement robust monitoring and logging mechanisms to track activities within OpenVAS. Monitor for unusual behavior, unauthorized access attempts, and system performance. Analyze logs regularly for security incidents.

8. Regular Backup and Recovery:

Establish a comprehensive backup and recovery strategy for OpenVAS configurations, scan results, and critical data. Regularly back up configurations to facilitate quick recovery in case of system failures or data loss.

9. Secure Configuration Files:

Protect sensitive configuration files and credentials associated with OpenVAS. Restrict file permissions to authorized users, and encrypt or hash stored credentials to prevent unauthorized access.

10. Secure the Underlying Operating System:

Secure the operating system hosting OpenVAS components. Follow best practices for securing the underlying Linux distribution, including regular security updates, minimizing unnecessary services, and configuring proper user access controls.

11. Regular Security Audits:

Conduct regular security audits of your OpenVAS deployment. Perform vulnerability assessments to identify and remediate potential weaknesses in the configuration, dependencies, or access controls.

12. Incident Response Plan:

Develop and maintain an incident response plan specific to OpenVAS. Establish procedures for responding to security incidents, such as unauthorized access or data breaches, to minimize the impact on your organization.

13. Follow Least Privilege Principle:

Apply the principle of least privilege to OpenVAS users and components. Grant only the minimum level of access necessary for each user or system component to perform its designated tasks.

14. Network Segmentation:

Consider segmenting your network to isolate OpenVAS components from critical production systems. This helps contain potential security incidents and limits the impact of compromised OpenVAS components.

15. Educate Users and Administrators:

Provide training and awareness programs for OpenVAS users and administrators. Educate them about security best practices, the importance of regular updates, and the potential risks associated with vulnerability assessments.

16. Engage with the OpenVAS Community:

Stay engaged with the OpenVAS community to stay informed about security updates, patches, and community-driven security discussions. Community engagement provides additional insights and support for addressing security concerns.

17. Regularly Review and Update Policies:

Periodically review and update security policies associated with OpenVAS. Ensure that policies align with evolving security requirements, organizational changes, and emerging threats.

18. Implement Two-Factor Authentication:

Enhance authentication security by implementing two-factor authentication for access to OpenVAS components. This additional layer of security adds an extra barrier against unauthorized access.

By adhering to these security considerations and precautions, you can enhance the overall security posture of your OpenVAS deployment. Taking proactive measures to secure access, communication, and configurations ensures that OpenVAS effectively contributes to your organization's cybersecurity efforts while minimizing potential risks.

9.3 Compliance and Regulatory Implications

OpenVAS plays a crucial role in helping organizations maintain a secure and compliant IT infrastructure. Adhering to compliance standards and regulatory requirements is essential for ensuring the protection of sensitive information and demonstrating a commitment to cybersecurity. Here are key compliance and regulatory implications associated with using OpenVAS:

1. General Data Protection Regulation (GDPR):

For organizations operating within the European Union or processing the personal data of EU residents, OpenVAS can assist in GDPR compliance. Regular vulnerability assessments help ensure the security of personal data, aligning with GDPR's data protection principles.

2. Health Insurance Portability and Accountability Act (HIPAA):

In healthcare environments, OpenVAS aids in maintaining HIPAA compliance by identifying and addressing vulnerabilities that could compromise the confidentiality, integrity, or availability of protected health information (PHI).

3. Payment Card Industry Data Security Standard (PCI DSS):

Organizations handling credit card transactions need to comply with PCI DSS. OpenVAS assists in identifying vulnerabilities in payment systems, ensuring compliance with PCI DSS requirements for securing cardholder data.

4. Federal Risk and Authorization Management Program (FedRAMP):

For organizations working with U.S. federal agencies, OpenVAS can contribute to compliance with FedRAMP requirements by identifying and mitigating vulnerabilities in cloud-based systems.

5. Sarbanes-Oxley Act (SOX):

OpenVAS aids organizations subject to SOX compliance by helping to identify and address vulnerabilities that could impact the integrity of financial reporting systems and data.

6. National Institute of Standards and Technology (NIST) Cybersecurity Framework:

Aligning with the NIST Cybersecurity Framework, OpenVAS assists organizations in identifying, protecting, detecting, responding to, and recovering from cybersecurity threats and vulnerabilities.

7. ISO/IEC 27001:

For organizations seeking ISO/IEC 27001 certification, OpenVAS supports the implementation of an information security management system (ISMS) by identifying and managing vulnerabilities in accordance with ISO/IEC 27001 controls.

8. Critical Infrastructure Protection (CIP) Standards:

In sectors such as energy and utilities, compliance with CIP standards is essential. OpenVAS aids in vulnerability assessments to ensure the security and resilience of critical infrastructure systems.

9. IT General Controls (ITGC):

For organizations subject to ITGC requirements, OpenVAS helps assess and strengthen general controls related to access controls, change management, and system security.

10. Data Protection Laws and Regulations:

Beyond GDPR, various countries and regions have specific data protection laws. OpenVAS supports compliance efforts by identifying vulnerabilities that could impact the security of personal and sensitive data.

11. Regulatory Compliance Reporting:

OpenVAS provides detailed reports that can be used for regulatory compliance reporting. These reports demonstrate the organization's commitment to identifying and mitigating cybersecurity risks.

12. Continuous Monitoring and Auditing:

Use OpenVAS for continuous monitoring and auditing of security controls. Regular vulnerability assessments contribute to ongoing compliance efforts and provide evidence for audits.

13. Documentation and Record-Keeping:

Maintain comprehensive documentation of OpenVAS configurations, scan results, and remediation efforts. Documentation is crucial for demonstrating due diligence in compliance and regulatory adherence.

14. Collaboration with Compliance Teams:

Collaborate with compliance teams to ensure that OpenVAS activities align with specific compliance requirements. Regular communication helps address any compliance-related concerns or evolving regulatory changes.

15. Vendor Security Requirements:

If your organization is subject to vendor security requirements, use OpenVAS to assess the security posture of third-party systems and applications, ensuring that vendors meet specified security standards.

By incorporating OpenVAS into your cybersecurity strategy, you can address compliance and regulatory requirements effectively. Regular vulnerability assessments, documentation practices, and collaboration with compliance teams contribute to a robust and compliant cybersecurity posture, instilling confidence in stakeholders and regulators alike.

10. Troubleshooting and Debugging

In the intricate dance between technology and security, hiccups and challenges are inevitable. Chapter 10 serves as your guide through the labyrinth of troubleshooting and debugging within OpenVAS—an indispensable skill set for any cybersecurity practitioner. As we explore common issues, decipher error messages, and unveil solutions, this chapter equips you with the tools needed to navigate the complexities of OpenVAS with resilience.

Common Issues and Solutions: Navigating the Roadblocks

The journey begins with an exploration of common issues encountered during OpenVAS operations. From connectivity glitches to configuration challenges, we dissect the roadblocks that may impede your vulnerability assessments. Each issue is met with a tailored solution, transforming obstacles into opportunities for learning and improvement.

Debugging Scan Failures: Unraveling the Mysteries

In the second subchapter, we delve into the art of debugging scan failures. A failed scan is not a setback but a puzzle waiting to be solved. Here, we guide you through the process of deciphering error messages, understanding scan logs, and effectively troubleshooting issues that might hinder the success of your vulnerability assessments.

Tips for Optimal Performance: Fine-Tuning Your Toolkit

The final subchapter unfolds a collection of tips for optimal performance. Beyond addressing issues, we explore proactive measures to fine-tune your OpenVAS toolkit for peak efficiency. From system optimizations to proactive monitoring, these tips empower you to not only troubleshoot problems but also prevent them, ensuring that your OpenVAS deployment remains robust and reliable.

As Chapter 10 unfolds, you will not only become adept at troubleshooting and debugging within OpenVAS but also gain insights into cultivating a resilient and responsive cybersecurity infrastructure. Join us in this exploration of challenges, where each resolution becomes a stepping stone towards OpenVAS mastery.

10.1 Common Issues and Solutions

While OpenVAS is a powerful tool for vulnerability assessment, users may encounter common issues during deployment and usage. Here are some common issues and their corresponding solutions:

1. Issue: Slow Scan Performance

Solution:

- Optimize scan configurations, adjusting settings like scan speed and concurrency to match the network environment.
- Ensure that OpenVAS is running on hardware with sufficient resources (CPU, memory) for the size of the scan.

2. Issue: False Positives/Negatives

Solution:

- Regularly update the OpenVAS database and plugins to access the latest vulnerability checks.
- Manually verify flagged vulnerabilities to reduce false positives and negatives.

3. Issue: Authentication Failures

Solution:

- Double-check and update authentication credentials for authenticated scans.
- Ensure that the scanning account has the necessary permissions on target systems.

4. Issue: Scan Interruption or Failure

Solution:

- Check system logs for any errors or crashes and address them accordingly.
- Increase resource allocation (CPU, memory) if scans are frequently interrupted due to resource limitations.

5. Issue: Outdated Plugins

Solution:

- Regularly update OpenVAS plugins to ensure that the system has the latest vulnerability checks.
- Configure OpenVAS to automatically update plugins.

6. Issue: Connectivity Problems

Solution:

- Verify network connectivity between OpenVAS components.
- Check firewalls and network configurations to ensure that required ports are open.

7. Issue: GPG Key Errors

Solution:

- Update GPG keys used for verifying plugin signatures.
- Ensure that the system clock is synchronized to prevent GPG key expiration errors.

8. Issue: Excessive Scan Load

Solution:

- Schedule scans during off-peak hours to reduce the impact on network and system performance.
- Adjust scan settings to control the scan load.

9. Issue: Incorrect Target Identification

Solution:

- Double-check target specifications in scan configurations, ensuring correct IP addresses and ranges.
- Validate DNS resolution for hostname-based targets.

10. Issue: Incomplete Scan Reports

Solution:

- Review OpenVAS logs for any errors during the scanning process.
- Adjust scan configurations to include all desired checks and increase verbosity if necessary.

11. Issue: Compatibility Problems

Solution:

- Check for compatibility issues with the OpenVAS version and the operating system. Update or patch if needed.
- Review release notes for known issues and solutions.

12. Issue: Web Interface Errors

Solution:

- Clear browser cache and cookies.
- Ensure that the browser is compatible with the OpenVAS web interface.

13. Issue: Database Corruption

Solution:

- Regularly backup the OpenVAS database.
- If corruption is suspected, restore from a known good backup.

14. Issue: Resource Exhaustion

Solution:

- Monitor system resource usage regularly and allocate additional resources if necessary.
- Optimize other running processes on the system to free up resources.

15. Issue: Lack of Documentation

Solution:

- Maintain comprehensive documentation for OpenVAS configurations, procedures, and issue resolution steps.

- Refer to official OpenVAS documentation and community forums for guidance.

Addressing common issues with OpenVAS requires a combination of careful configuration, routine maintenance, and troubleshooting. Regularly staying informed about updates, maintaining documentation, and actively participating in the OpenVAS community can contribute to a more seamless and effective usage experience.

10.2 Debugging Scan Failures

Encountering scan failures in OpenVAS can be frustrating, but effective debugging can help identify and resolve issues promptly. Here's a systematic approach to debugging scan failures:

1. Check System Logs:

- Examine system logs for any error messages related to OpenVAS. Logs are often located in /var/log/openvas/ or similar directories.
- Look for information on crashes, errors, or other issues that may have occurred during the scan.

2. Review OpenVAS Logs:

- Access OpenVAS logs through the Greenbone Security Assistant (GSA) or command-line interface.
- Check for any scan-related errors, warnings, or anomalies reported by OpenVAS components.

3. Verify Connectivity:

- Ensure that there are no network connectivity issues between OpenVAS components.
- Confirm that the target systems are reachable from the OpenVAS scanner.

4. Check Target Specifications:

- Review the target specifications in the scan configuration. Verify that IP addresses, hostnames, and ranges are correctly defined.
- Ensure that DNS resolution is working correctly for hostname-based targets.

5. Authentication Issues:

- If the scan involves authentication, double-check the credentials used for scanning.
- Ensure that the scanning account has the necessary permissions on the target systems.

6. Resource Allocation:

- Assess system resource utilization during the scan. Examine CPU, memory, and disk usage to identify potential bottlenecks.
- Increase resource allocation if the scan fails due to resource exhaustion.

7. Update Plugins:

- Regularly update OpenVAS plugins to ensure that the system has the latest vulnerability checks.
- Confirm that plugin updates are successful and do not encounter errors.

8. Review Scan Configuration:

- Validate the scan configuration settings, including target exclusions, scan types, and scan policies.
- Adjust configurations to include necessary checks and address any inconsistencies.

9. Check for Dependencies:

- Ensure that any external dependencies, such as required libraries or utilities, are installed and up to date.
- Review OpenVAS documentation for information on specific dependencies.

10. Web Interface Errors:

- If scan failures are reported through the web interface, check for specific error messages.
- Clear browser cache and cookies, and try accessing the web interface using a different browser.

11. GPG Key Verification:

- Verify the GPG keys used for verifying plugin signatures. Update keys if necessary.
- Confirm that the system clock is synchronized to prevent GPG key-related errors.

12. Scan Policy Review:

- Review the scan policies associated with the failed scan. Ensure that the policies are appropriate for the target environment.
- Modify policies based on the specific requirements of the scan.

13. Check for Known Issues:

- Consult OpenVAS release notes and community forums for information on known issues related to the OpenVAS version you are using.
- Look for patches or workarounds for any identified issues.

14. Run Manual Tests:

- Manually test the connectivity to target systems from the OpenVAS scanner.
- Conduct isolated scans with minimal configurations to identify specific components causing issues.

15. Engage with the Community:

- Seek assistance from the OpenVAS community through forums and discussion groups.
- Share details of the scan failure, logs, and any error messages for community input.

16. Review Documentation:

- Refer to official OpenVAS documentation for troubleshooting guidance.
- Explore documentation on common scan failures and solutions provided by the OpenVAS community.

17. Implement Remediations:

- Apply identified solutions and remediations based on the analysis of logs and diagnostic information.
- Monitor subsequent scans to ensure that the issues have been resolved.

Debugging scan failures in OpenVAS requires a methodical approach, involving a thorough review of logs, configurations, and potential issues. By systematically addressing each aspect, users can identify the root cause of scan failures and implement effective solutions. Active engagement with the OpenVAS community and staying informed about updates contribute to a more successful resolution of scan-related issues.

10.3 Tips for Optimal Performance

OpenVAS, the Open Vulnerability Assessment System, is a powerful tool widely used for identifying and managing security vulnerabilities in IT environments. To ensure optimal performance and efficiency in vulnerability assessments, it's crucial to implement best practices and tips that streamline the scanning process, enhance accuracy, and minimize resource utilization. In this comprehensive guide, we'll delve into key strategies for achieving optimal performance in OpenVAS.

1. Regular Updates for Robust Security:

Keeping OpenVAS components up to date is fundamental to maintaining a strong security posture. Regular updates encompass not only the OpenVAS software itself but also plugins, scripts, and vulnerability feeds. These updates are critical to staying abreast of the latest threats and ensuring that the system is equipped with the most recent security checks and improvements.

2. Fine-Tune Scan Configurations:

Tailoring scan configurations to the specifics of your network environment is paramount. OpenVAS offers a range of parameters that can be adjusted to optimize scan speed, concurrency, and target exclusions. A thoughtful configuration that aligns with the size and complexity of your infrastructure enhances the accuracy and relevance of vulnerability assessments.

3. Strategic Scan Scheduling:

Plan and schedule scans during off-peak hours to minimize disruption to regular business operations. This not only reduces the impact on network bandwidth but also ensures that critical systems are not overwhelmed during the scanning process. Strategic scheduling is particularly important for large-scale assessments.

4. Leverage Authenticated Scans:

Authenticated scans provide a more comprehensive view of your systems' security posture by conducting scans with valid credentials. This allows OpenVAS to access deeper layers of the infrastructure, uncovering vulnerabilities that might remain hidden during external scans. Authenticated scans enhance the accuracy of results and contribute to a more robust security assessment.

5. Prioritize High-Impact Vulnerabilities:

Efficient vulnerability management involves prioritizing remediation efforts based on the severity and potential impact of identified vulnerabilities. Focus on addressing high-impact vulnerabilities first to mitigate the most critical risks to your organization. This targeted approach ensures that resources are allocated to the areas of greatest concern.

6. Optimize Resource Allocation:

Monitoring and optimizing system resource usage are key factors in achieving optimal OpenVAS performance. Keep a close eye on CPU, memory, and disk utilization during scans. This proactive approach enables you to identify potential bottlenecks and allocate additional resources as needed. Optimizing resource allocation enhances the overall efficiency of the vulnerability assessment process.

7. Consider Distributed Architecture:

For large-scale environments, consider implementing a distributed architecture for OpenVAS. Distributing the workload across multiple scanners and managers can significantly enhance scan performance and reduce the time required for assessments. This approach is particularly beneficial for organizations with extensive and geographically dispersed IT infrastructures.

8. Implement Scan Exclusions Strategically:

Strategically exclude non-essential systems or portions of the network from certain scans to improve efficiency. By excluding systems that do not require frequent assessments or are known to be free of vulnerabilities, you can streamline the scanning process and focus resources on critical areas.

9. Utilize Performance-Optimized NASL Scripts:

Nessus Attack Scripting Language (NASL) scripts play a crucial role in vulnerability checks performed by OpenVAS. Utilize performance-optimized NASL scripts to enhance scan efficiency. Well-crafted scripts can reduce scan times and resource consumption while ensuring thorough vulnerability coverage.

10. Monitor and Analyze Scan Reports Regularly:

The value of OpenVAS lies not just in running scans but also in the insightful analysis of scan reports. Regularly review and analyze scan reports to identify trends, track improvements, and make informed decisions regarding vulnerability remediation. Monitoring reports provides actionable insights for enhancing overall security.

11. Optimize Database Configuration:

The performance of OpenVAS is closely tied to the efficiency of its underlying database. Optimize the database configuration, considering factors such as indexing, storage, and query optimization. A well-tuned database contributes to faster scan execution and responsive reporting.

12. Implement Automated Scanning Workflows:

Automation is a key element in achieving efficiency in vulnerability assessments. Implement automated scanning workflows to streamline repetitive tasks such as scan launches, report generation, and result analysis. Automation not only saves time but also ensures consistency in scanning processes.

13. Maintain Comprehensive Documentation:

Documenting configurations, scan policies, and best practices is crucial for maintaining a structured and organized OpenVAS environment. Comprehensive documentation aids in troubleshooting, knowledge transfer among team members, and ensures that established best practices are consistently followed.

14. Engage with the OpenVAS Community:

The OpenVAS community serves as a valuable resource for users seeking guidance and solutions. Engage with the community through forums, discussion groups, and other channels. Sharing experiences, seeking advice, and staying informed about community-driven insights contribute to a more informed and effective use of OpenVAS.

15. Conduct Regular Training for Users:

Educating users on the nuances of OpenVAS and cybersecurity best practices is essential. Regular training sessions ensure that users are well-equipped to utilize OpenVAS effectively, interpret scan reports, and contribute to the organization's overall cybersecurity efforts.

Optimizing OpenVAS performance is a multifaceted endeavor that involves a combination of thoughtful configuration, strategic scheduling, resource management, and continuous improvement. By adhering to these tips and best practices, organizations can harness the full potential of OpenVAS for comprehensive vulnerability assessments, leading to enhanced cybersecurity resilience and proactive risk management. As the threat landscape evolves, staying committed to optimizing OpenVAS ensures that organizations can adapt and respond effectively to emerging security challenges.

11. Integration with Security Workflows

In the orchestration of a robust cybersecurity strategy, the integration of tools into cohesive workflows is paramount. Chapter 11 unfolds the transformative potential of OpenVAS as it seamlessly blends into broader security workflows. Here, we explore the synergies between OpenVAS and other security tools, creating a unified defense strategy that is agile, responsive, and comprehensive.

Connecting OpenVAS with SIEM Tools: The Synergy of Information

The journey begins with the first subchapter, where we delve into the integration of OpenVAS with Security Information and Event Management (SIEM) tools. By uniting the capabilities of OpenVAS with the analytical power of SIEM, you can create a dynamic synergy that not only identifies vulnerabilities but also contextualizes them within the broader security landscape. This integration fosters a proactive approach to threat detection and response.

Collaboration with Incident Response Teams: Unifying Defenses

In the second subchapter, we explore the collaborative potential of OpenVAS within incident response teams. OpenVAS is not a solitary tool but a cooperative force that, when integrated seamlessly into incident response workflows, enhances the speed and efficiency of mitigating vulnerabilities. We unravel strategies for fostering collaboration, ensuring that OpenVAS becomes an integral component of your incident response arsenal.

Incorporating OpenVAS into Cybersecurity Strategies: A Holistic Approach

The final subchapter expands our view to the holistic incorporation of OpenVAS into overarching cybersecurity strategies. Here, we explore how OpenVAS aligns with broader cybersecurity initiatives, from risk management to threat intelligence. By understanding the role of OpenVAS within the larger context, you can craft a comprehensive strategy that addresses vulnerabilities as part of a strategic, proactive defense.

As Chapter 11 unfolds, you will not only grasp the technical aspects of integration but also internalize the strategic considerations that make OpenVAS an indispensable component of your cybersecurity ecosystem. Join us in this exploration of synergy, where each integration propels your defenses to new heights.

11.1 Connecting OpenVAS with SIEM Tools

In the dynamic landscape of cybersecurity, integrating security tools is crucial for organizations to enhance their ability to detect, respond to, and mitigate threats effectively. One powerful integration is between OpenVAS (Open Vulnerability Assessment System) and Security Information and Event Management (SIEM) tools. This integration allows for seamless information sharing, providing a comprehensive security solution. In this guide, we'll explore the benefits and steps involved in connecting OpenVAS with SIEM tools.

Benefits of Connecting OpenVAS with SIEM:

Unified Threat Visibility:

Integration enables a consolidated view of both vulnerabilities identified by OpenVAS and real-time security events collected by the SIEM tool. This unified visibility enhances the overall understanding of the security landscape.

Correlation of Events and Vulnerabilities:

SIEM tools excel in event correlation. By connecting OpenVAS, organizations can correlate vulnerability scan results with security events. This correlation provides context to potential threats and aids in prioritizing responses.

Streamlined Incident Response:

Integrating OpenVAS with SIEM facilitates streamlined incident response. When vulnerabilities are identified, the SIEM tool can trigger predefined responses, ensuring a rapid and coordinated reaction to potential security risks.

Enhanced Reporting and Analysis:

Combined data from OpenVAS and SIEM tools offers richer reporting and analysis capabilities. Security teams can generate comprehensive reports that not only detail vulnerabilities but also provide insights into the broader threat landscape.

Automation of Remediation:

SIEM integration enables the automation of remediation processes. Security teams can configure automated responses based on the severity of vulnerabilities, reducing manual intervention and accelerating the mitigation of risks.

Steps to Connect OpenVAS with SIEM Tools:

Connecting OpenVAS with a SIEM tool involves configuring both systems to share information. The steps below outline the general process, though specifics may vary based on the SIEM tool used.

1. Identify Compatible SIEM Tool:

Choose a SIEM tool that is compatible with OpenVAS. Common SIEM tools include Splunk, ELK Stack (Elasticsearch, Logstash, Kibana), ArcSight, and others.

2. Install and Configure SIEM Tool:

Install and configure the chosen SIEM tool. Follow the specific documentation provided by the SIEM tool vendor for installation steps and initial setup.

3. Configure OpenVAS for Logging:

Configure OpenVAS to generate logs in a format compatible with the SIEM tool. This may involve adjusting logging settings within OpenVAS to ensure that relevant information is recorded.

4. Set Up Log Forwarding:

Configure OpenVAS to forward logs to the SIEM tool. This typically involves specifying the SIEM tool's IP address or hostname and defining the communication protocol (e.g., syslog, SNMP).

5. Configure SIEM Tool to Ingest OpenVAS Logs:

In the SIEM tool, create configurations to ingest logs from OpenVAS. This may involve defining data sources, log formats, and protocols for receiving OpenVAS data.

6. Define Correlation Rules:

Establish correlation rules within the SIEM tool to correlate OpenVAS vulnerability scan results with other security events. This step enhances the context of vulnerabilities within the broader security context.

7. Configure Automated Responses:

Leverage the SIEM tool's capabilities to configure automated responses based on OpenVAS scan results. Automated responses can include alerting, blocking, or triggering remediation processes.

8. Test and Validate Integration:

Conduct thorough testing to ensure the seamless flow of information between OpenVAS and the SIEM tool. Validate that vulnerabilities detected by OpenVAS are accurately reflected in the SIEM tool's interface.

9. Monitor and Fine-Tune:

Continuously monitor the integration to identify any issues or discrepancies. Fine-tune correlation rules and automated responses based on the evolving threat landscape and organizational requirements.

Considerations and Best Practices:

Security and Access Controls:

Implement strong security measures and access controls to protect the integrity of the integration. Ensure that only authorized personnel have access to OpenVAS and the SIEM tool configurations.

Regular Updates and Maintenance:

Keep both OpenVAS and the SIEM tool up to date with the latest patches and updates. Regular maintenance ensures that the integration remains robust and secure.

Documentation:

Maintain comprehensive documentation outlining the integration process, configurations, and any customizations made. Documentation is invaluable for troubleshooting and knowledge transfer.

Collaboration Between Teams:

Foster collaboration between the teams responsible for managing OpenVAS and the SIEM tool. Effective communication ensures that both tools work in harmony to strengthen the organization's security posture.

Connecting OpenVAS with SIEM tools is a strategic move toward creating a more unified and responsive cybersecurity ecosystem. By integrating vulnerability assessment capabilities with real-time event monitoring, organizations can enhance their ability to detect and address security threats promptly. This collaboration between OpenVAS and SIEM tools contributes to a more resilient and proactive approach to cybersecurity, aligning with the dynamic nature of modern digital environments.

11.2 Collaboration with Incident Response Teams

In the complex landscape of cybersecurity, collaboration is key to mounting effective responses to threats. The integration of OpenVAS (Open Vulnerability Assessment System) with incident response teams plays a critical role in fortifying an organization's security posture. This collaboration ensures that vulnerabilities identified by OpenVAS are swiftly addressed, minimizing the potential impact of security incidents. In this guide, we'll explore the benefits and steps involved in fostering collaboration between OpenVAS and incident response teams.

Benefits of Collaboration with Incident Response Teams:

Rapid Response to Critical Vulnerabilities:

Incident response teams are equipped to swiftly respond to critical vulnerabilities identified by OpenVAS. This collaboration ensures that high-impact vulnerabilities are addressed promptly to mitigate potential risks.

Contextual Understanding of Threats:

Incident response teams bring a contextual understanding of threats to the table. By collaborating with OpenVAS, they gain insights into the organization's vulnerability landscape, enabling more informed incident response strategies.

Streamlined Communication:

Seamless communication between OpenVAS and incident response teams streamlines the flow of information. Incident responders can receive real-time updates on vulnerabilities, enabling them to prioritize and tailor their responses effectively.

Automated Remediation Workflows:

Collaboration allows for the implementation of automated remediation workflows. Incident response teams can configure automated responses based on OpenVAS scan results, optimizing the remediation process and reducing manual intervention.

Continuous Monitoring and Adaptation:

Incident response teams, in collaboration with OpenVAS, can continuously monitor the threat landscape. This proactive approach enables organizations to adapt to evolving threats, ensuring that security measures remain effective.

Steps for Collaborating with Incident Response Teams:

1. Establish Clear Communication Channels:

Create clear communication channels between OpenVAS administrators and incident response teams. Establish protocols for sharing vulnerability information, incident reports, and response strategies.

2. Define Incident Severity Levels:

Work collaboratively to define incident severity levels based on OpenVAS scan results. This classification helps incident response teams prioritize their efforts and respond swiftly to critical vulnerabilities.

3. Integrate OpenVAS with Incident Response Platforms:

Integrate OpenVAS with incident response platforms, if applicable. This integration allows for the automatic generation of incidents and alerts based on OpenVAS scan results, streamlining the incident response workflow.

4. Conduct Joint Training Exercises:

Conduct joint training exercises involving OpenVAS administrators and incident response teams. These exercises enhance the teams' understanding of each other's workflows, fostering a collaborative and efficient response culture.

5. Share Threat Intelligence:

Establish mechanisms for sharing threat intelligence between OpenVAS and incident response teams. This collaborative sharing of information enhances the overall threat visibility and facilitates more effective incident detection and response.

6. Implement Automated Incident Response Playbooks:

Collaboratively develop and implement automated incident response playbooks that incorporate OpenVAS scan results. Automated playbooks can include predefined responses to common vulnerabilities, reducing response times.

7. Regularly Review and Update Response Plans:

Collaborate on the regular review and update of incident response plans based on the evolving threat landscape and changes in the organization's infrastructure. Ensure that OpenVAS findings are consistently integrated into these plans.

8. Establish Incident Escalation Procedures:

Define incident escalation procedures that clearly outline when and how OpenVAS scan results should be escalated to incident response teams. This ensures that critical vulnerabilities receive immediate attention.

9. Facilitate Cross-Team Collaboration:

Create opportunities for cross-team collaboration through joint meetings, workshops, and collaborative platforms. This fosters a sense of shared responsibility and encourages the exchange of knowledge and expertise.

10. Document Collaboration Procedures:

Document collaboration procedures between OpenVAS and incident response teams. This documentation should include contact information, escalation paths, incident response workflows, and any specific processes related to OpenVAS findings.

Considerations and Best Practices:

Security and Access Controls:

Implement robust security measures and access controls to safeguard information shared between OpenVAS and incident response teams. Ensure that sensitive data is only accessible to authorized personnel.

Continuous Improvement:

Foster a culture of continuous improvement. Regularly assess the effectiveness of collaboration efforts, seeking feedback from both OpenVAS administrators and incident response teams to identify areas for enhancement.

Incident Simulation Exercises:

Conduct incident simulation exercises that involve OpenVAS scan results. These exercises help teams practice coordinated responses to specific vulnerabilities and ensure that response plans are well-executed.

Cultural Alignment:

Ensure that there is a cultural alignment between OpenVAS administrators and incident response teams. A shared commitment to security goals and a collaborative mindset are essential for effective collaboration.

Collaboration between OpenVAS and incident response teams is instrumental in fortifying an organization's cybersecurity defenses. By establishing clear communication channels, integrating workflows, and fostering a culture of collaboration, organizations can effectively respond to vulnerabilities identified by OpenVAS, minimizing the risk of security incidents. This collaborative approach reflects a proactive and resilient stance in the face of evolving cyber threats, ultimately contributing to a more secure and resilient digital environment.

11.3 Incorporating OpenVAS into Cybersecurity Strategies

In the ever-evolving landscape of cybersecurity, organizations must adopt a comprehensive approach to identify, assess, and mitigate vulnerabilities effectively. OpenVAS (Open Vulnerability Assessment System) serves as a potent tool for vulnerability management, contributing to the overall cybersecurity strategy. In this guide, we'll explore the key considerations and steps involved in incorporating OpenVAS into cybersecurity strategies for enhanced resilience against evolving threats.

Benefits of Incorporating OpenVAS:

Proactive Vulnerability Identification:

OpenVAS enables organizations to proactively identify and assess vulnerabilities in their IT infrastructure. This proactive approach allows for early detection and mitigation, reducing the risk of exploitation.

Comprehensive Vulnerability Scanning:

The comprehensive scanning capabilities of OpenVAS cover a wide range of vulnerabilities, including common vulnerabilities and exposures (CVEs). This breadth ensures that organizations have a holistic view of their security posture.

Prioritization of Remediation Efforts:

OpenVAS provides severity assessments for identified vulnerabilities, allowing organizations to prioritize remediation efforts. This strategic prioritization ensures that critical vulnerabilities are addressed first, optimizing resource allocation.

Continuous Monitoring and Reporting:

Incorporating OpenVAS into cybersecurity strategies enables continuous monitoring of the organization's security landscape. Automated reporting features provide real-time insights, supporting informed decision-making and policy adjustments.

Integration with Incident Response:

OpenVAS seamlessly integrates with incident response workflows. The collaboration between vulnerability assessments and incident response enhances the organization's ability to detect, respond to, and mitigate potential security incidents.

Steps to Incorporate OpenVAS into Cybersecurity Strategies:

1. Define Clear Objectives:

Clearly define the objectives of incorporating OpenVAS into the cybersecurity strategy. Whether the focus is on compliance, risk reduction, or overall security enhancement, establishing clear goals is crucial.

2. Conduct Initial Vulnerability Assessments:

Perform initial vulnerability assessments using OpenVAS to establish a baseline of the organization's security posture. This assessment identifies existing vulnerabilities and forms the basis for subsequent risk management efforts.

3. Develop a Risk Management Plan:

Based on OpenVAS scan results, develop a risk management plan that outlines strategies for prioritizing, mitigating, or accepting identified vulnerabilities. This plan should align with the organization's risk tolerance and business objectives.

4. Integrate with Patch Management:

Integrate OpenVAS with patch management processes. The collaboration between vulnerability assessment and patch management ensures a streamlined approach to addressing identified vulnerabilities promptly.

5. Establish Continuous Monitoring:

Implement continuous monitoring using OpenVAS to regularly assess and reassess the organization's security posture. Continuous monitoring allows for the identification of new vulnerabilities and ensures that the security strategy remains adaptive.

6. Implement Automated Scanning Workflows:

Leverage automated scanning workflows within OpenVAS to streamline the vulnerability assessment process. Automation accelerates the scanning process and allows for regular assessments without manual intervention.

7. Train Security Personnel:

Provide training to security personnel on the effective use of OpenVAS. This includes understanding scan results, interpreting severity assessments, and integrating OpenVAS findings into overall security decision-making processes.

8. Align with Compliance Requirements:

Align the use of OpenVAS with compliance requirements applicable to the organization. Ensure that vulnerability assessments performed by OpenVAS contribute to meeting regulatory standards and industry best practices.

9. Foster Collaboration Across Teams:

Foster collaboration across IT, security, and development teams. OpenVAS findings should be communicated effectively to relevant stakeholders, and collaboration is essential for implementing remediation efforts.

10. Establish Incident Response Integration:

Integrate OpenVAS with incident response processes. Ensure that vulnerabilities identified by OpenVAS trigger appropriate responses within the incident response workflow, facilitating a coordinated approach to security incidents.

Considerations and Best Practices:

Regularly Update OpenVAS Components:

Keep OpenVAS components, including software, plugins, and vulnerability feeds, up to date. Regular updates ensure that the tool is equipped with the latest security checks and improvements.

Document Processes and Procedures:

Maintain comprehensive documentation outlining the processes and procedures related to incorporating OpenVAS into the cybersecurity strategy. This documentation aids in training, auditing, and knowledge transfer.

Monitor Performance and Efficiency:

Regularly monitor the performance and efficiency of OpenVAS scans. Assess scan results, identify any issues, and make adjustments to configurations or workflows to optimize performance.

Engage with the OpenVAS Community:

Stay actively engaged with the OpenVAS community. The community provides valuable insights, updates, and support that can enhance the effectiveness of OpenVAS within the cybersecurity strategy.

Incorporating OpenVAS into cybersecurity strategies is a strategic decision that contributes to the organization's overall resilience against cyber threats. By defining clear objectives, developing risk management plans, and fostering collaboration, organizations can leverage the comprehensive capabilities of OpenVAS for proactive vulnerability management. This integration aligns with industry best practices, compliance requirements, and a proactive stance in the face of evolving cybersecurity challenges.

12. Case Studies and Real-World Examples

In the world of cybersecurity, theory finds its true test in the crucible of real-world scenarios. Chapter 12 invites you to embark on a journey through tangible applications of OpenVAS, exploring case studies and real-world examples that unveil the tool's prowess in diverse and dynamic environments. Through these narratives, we extract lessons, unveil success stories, and illuminate the practical impact of mastering OpenVAS.

Application of OpenVAS in Scenario A: Unraveling Complexities

Our journey begins with the first subchapter, where we unravel the intricate tapestry of OpenVAS in a specific scenario. From initial setup to the resolution of challenges, we dissect the application of OpenVAS in a complex environment, providing insights into the decision-making process, the effectiveness of the tool, and the transformative impact on cybersecurity defenses.

Success Stories and Lessons Learned: Insights from the Field

In the second subchapter, we delve into success stories—instances where OpenVAS became a stalwart guardian in the face of real-world threats. These stories go beyond technical details, encapsulating the strategic decisions, collaborative efforts, and resilience that led to triumph. Embedded within each success story are valuable lessons that you can carry forward in your own journey of mastering OpenVAS.

As Chapter 12 unfolds, you will not only witness OpenVAS in action but also draw inspiration and knowledge from real-world applications. Join us in this exploration of case studies, where theory meets practice, and where the lines between hypothetical and actual blur in the dynamic realm of cybersecurity.

12.1 Application of OpenVAS in Scenario A

In Scenario A, we'll explore the application of OpenVAS (Open Vulnerability Assessment System) in the context of a Network Infrastructure Security Assessment. This scenario involves a mid-sized enterprise with a diverse network infrastructure consisting of servers, routers, switches, and various endpoints. The organization is keen on identifying and addressing vulnerabilities within its network to enhance overall security. OpenVAS will be utilized to conduct a comprehensive assessment and provide actionable insights.

Scenario A Overview:

Organization Profile:

Type: Mid-sized enterprise.

Infrastructure: Diverse network including servers, routers, switches, and endpoints.
Objective: Identify and address vulnerabilities in the network infrastructure.

Application of OpenVAS:

1. Initial Discovery and Scoping:

Utilize OpenVAS to perform an initial discovery of all devices within the network. This includes servers, routers, switches, and endpoints. Scoping involves defining the range of IP addresses and identifying potential entry points for assessments.

2. Vulnerability Scanning:

Conduct a comprehensive vulnerability scan using OpenVAS. This involves identifying known vulnerabilities, misconfigurations, and potential security weaknesses across the network infrastructure. OpenVAS employs a vast database of vulnerability checks to assess each device thoroughly.

3. Prioritization of Vulnerabilities:

Leverage OpenVAS's severity assessments to prioritize identified vulnerabilities based on their potential impact. This step ensures that the organization focuses on addressing the most critical security risks first.

4. Report Generation:

Generate detailed reports using OpenVAS to document the findings of the vulnerability assessment. Reports should include an overview of vulnerabilities, their severity levels, and recommended remediation actions. These reports serve as a valuable resource for decision-making and communication.

5. Collaboration with IT and Security Teams:

Foster collaboration between IT and security teams to interpret OpenVAS scan results. Security teams can provide insights into the potential implications of vulnerabilities, while IT teams play a key role in implementing remediation measures.

6. Patch Management Integration:

Integrate OpenVAS with the organization's patch management processes. The collaboration ensures that vulnerabilities identified by OpenVAS align with the patching strategy, streamlining the remediation process.

7. Continuous Monitoring:

Establish continuous monitoring using OpenVAS to regularly reassess the network infrastructure for new vulnerabilities. Continuous monitoring ensures that the organization remains proactive in addressing emerging security threats.

8. Incident Response Integration:

Integrate OpenVAS with incident response workflows. When critical vulnerabilities are identified, OpenVAS triggers incident response mechanisms, ensuring a coordinated approach to addressing and mitigating potential security incidents.

9. Compliance Alignment:

Align the use of OpenVAS with regulatory and compliance requirements applicable to the organization. This ensures that the vulnerability assessments contribute to maintaining a secure and compliant network infrastructure.

10. Documentation and Training:

Document processes and procedures related to the application of OpenVAS in the network infrastructure security assessment. Conduct training sessions for relevant personnel to enhance their understanding of OpenVAS and its role in cybersecurity.

Considerations and Best Practices:

Regular Updates:

Ensure that OpenVAS components, including software, plugins, and vulnerability feeds, are regularly updated to leverage the latest security checks and improvements.

Customization of Scans:

Customize OpenVAS scans based on the specific requirements and nuances of the organization's network infrastructure. Tailoring scans enhances the relevance and accuracy of vulnerability assessments.

Engage with the OpenVAS Community:

Actively engage with the OpenVAS community to stay informed about updates, best practices, and community-driven insights. The community serves as a valuable resource for users implementing OpenVAS in diverse scenarios.

In Scenario A, the application of OpenVAS in a Network Infrastructure Security Assessment provides the organization with a powerful tool to proactively identify and address vulnerabilities. By integrating OpenVAS into the cybersecurity strategy, the organization can maintain a robust security posture, align with compliance requirements, and foster collaboration between IT and security teams. The continuous monitoring and incident response integration further contribute to a resilient approach in addressing evolving cybersecurity challenges within the network infrastructure.

12.2 Success Stories and Lessons Learned

In the realm of cybersecurity, success stories and lessons learned are invaluable in shaping effective practices and strategies. This section delves into real-world success stories of organizations that have applied OpenVAS (Open Vulnerability Assessment System) in diverse scenarios, highlighting key achievements and lessons gleaned from their experiences.

Success Story 1: Financial Institution Fortifies Network Security

Organization Profile:

Type: Large financial institution.

Challenge: Addressing vulnerabilities across a complex network infrastructure.

Solution: Implemented OpenVAS for regular vulnerability assessments.

Key Achievements:

Comprehensive Visibility:

OpenVAS provided the financial institution with comprehensive visibility into vulnerabilities across servers, databases, and network devices. The organization gained a clear understanding of its risk landscape.

Risk-Based Prioritization:

Leveraging OpenVAS's severity assessments, the institution prioritized vulnerabilities based on risk. This risk-based approach enabled efficient resource allocation for remediation efforts, focusing on the most critical issues first.

Integration with Patch Management:

Successful integration of OpenVAS with the organization's patch management processes streamlined the remediation workflow.

Identified vulnerabilities seamlessly aligned with the patching strategy, reducing the time to remediate.

Continuous Monitoring:

Continuous monitoring using OpenVAS allowed the financial institution to stay ahead of emerging threats. Regular vulnerability assessments ensured that the organization proactively addressed new vulnerabilities as they emerged.

Lessons Learned:

Customize Scans for Specific Environments:

The financial institution emphasized the importance of customizing OpenVAS scans to match the specific characteristics of its diverse environment. Tailoring scans enhanced the relevance and accuracy of vulnerability assessments.

Engage Cross-Functional Teams:

Successful vulnerability management required collaboration between security and IT teams. Engaging both teams ensured a holistic understanding of vulnerabilities and effective collaboration in remediation efforts.

Success Story 2: Technology Firm Enhances Cloud Security

Organization Profile:

- **Type**: Technology firm with a cloud-based infrastructure.
- **Challenge**: Securing cloud assets and identifying misconfigurations.
- **Solution**: Implemented OpenVAS for cloud-specific vulnerability assessments.

Key Achievements:

Cloud-Specific Assessments:

OpenVAS was configured to perform cloud-specific vulnerability assessments. The technology firm gained insights into misconfigurations, insecure storage settings, and other cloud-specific issues that traditional scans might overlook.

Automated Remediation Workflows:

The integration of OpenVAS with automated remediation workflows allowed the firm to address identified vulnerabilities swiftly. Automated responses were configured based on OpenVAS scan results, reducing manual intervention.

Real-Time Reporting:

OpenVAS provided real-time reporting on vulnerabilities within the cloud environment. This transparency empowered the organization to make informed decisions promptly, ensuring the security of cloud assets.

Lessons Learned:

Stay Abreast of Cloud Security Best Practices:

The technology firm highlighted the importance of staying abreast of cloud security best practices. Adapting OpenVAS configurations to align with evolving cloud security standards was crucial for effective assessments.

Embrace Automation for Swift Responses:

Leveraging automation for remediation processes allowed the firm to respond swiftly to vulnerabilities. This approach ensured that misconfigurations and security issues were addressed in near real-time.

Common Lessons Across Success Stories:

Continuous Learning and Adaptation:

Both organizations emphasized the need for continuous learning and adaptation. The dynamic nature of cybersecurity requires organizations to stay informed about emerging threats, vulnerabilities, and best practices.

Documentation and Knowledge Transfer:

Documenting processes and lessons learned was critical for knowledge transfer within the organizations. Comprehensive documentation facilitated training sessions, audits, and the seamless transfer of expertise.

Engagement with the OpenVAS Community:

Both success stories highlighted the importance of actively engaging with the OpenVAS community. Leveraging community-driven insights, updates, and support enhanced the effectiveness of OpenVAS implementations.

The success stories of applying OpenVAS in real-world scenarios underscore its versatility and effectiveness in addressing diverse cybersecurity challenges. The lessons learned from these experiences emphasize the importance of customization, collaboration, continuous learning, and community engagement. Organizations leveraging OpenVAS not only fortify their security postures but also contribute to the collective knowledge and resilience of the cybersecurity community.

13. Future Trends in Vulnerability Assessment

As the digital landscape continues to evolve, so too must our approaches to cybersecurity. Chapter 13 invites you to gaze into the crystal ball of vulnerability assessment, exploring the emerging trends that will shape the future of OpenVAS and its role in safeguarding digital ecosystems. From cutting-edge technologies to evolving threat vectors, this chapter provides a glimpse into the landscape that lies beyond the horizon.

Emerging Technologies and Their Impact: The Next Frontier

Our journey begins with the exploration of emerging technologies that are poised to reshape vulnerability assessment. From artificial intelligence and machine learning to advancements in network architectures, we unravel the potential impact of these technologies on the capabilities of OpenVAS and its ability to adapt to novel challenges.

Evolving Threats and OpenVAS's Role in Mitigation: A Dynamic Partnership

In the second subchapter, we delve into the evolving threat landscape. As cyber threats morph and diversify, OpenVAS stands as a stalwart sentinel. Here, we explore how OpenVAS can adapt to new threat vectors, evolving attack methodologies, and the shifting terrain of cybersecurity. Understanding the future threatscape is crucial for preparing OpenVAS as a resilient guardian.

As Chapter 13 unfolds, you will peer into the future of vulnerability assessment, envisioning the role OpenVAS will play in securing digital landscapes yet to unfold. Join us in this exploration of future trends, where anticipation and adaptation become the keys to staying ahead in the dynamic realm of cybersecurity.

13.1 Emerging Technologies and Their Impact

In the ever-evolving landscape of cybersecurity, emerging technologies play a pivotal role in shaping the future of vulnerability assessment practices. This section explores key emerging technologies and their impact on the field of vulnerability assessment, providing insights into how these advancements are reshaping approaches to identifying and mitigating security risks.

1. Artificial Intelligence (AI) and Machine Learning (ML):

Impact:

Automated Threat Detection:

AI and ML algorithms enhance the automation of threat detection in vulnerability assessments. These technologies can analyze vast datasets to identify patterns, anomalies, and potential security risks more efficiently than traditional methods.

Behavioral Analysis:

AI-driven behavioral analysis adds a layer of sophistication to vulnerability assessments. By learning normal system behaviors, AI can detect deviations that may indicate the presence of vulnerabilities or malicious activities.

Predictive Analytics:

Predictive analytics powered by AI allows organizations to anticipate potential vulnerabilities based on historical data and emerging trends. This proactive approach enables timely preventive measures.

2. Internet of Things (IoT):

Impact:

Extended Attack Surface:

The proliferation of IoT devices expands the attack surface, requiring vulnerability assessments to cover a broader range of endpoints. Assessments must consider the unique security challenges posed by IoT devices and their ecosystems.

Embedded Security Assessments:

Vulnerability assessments now extend beyond traditional IT infrastructure to include embedded systems in IoT devices. Assessors need to evaluate not only software vulnerabilities but also potential weaknesses in hardware components.

3. Cloud Computing:

Impact:

Dynamic Infrastructure:

Cloud environments introduce dynamic and elastic infrastructure, challenging traditional vulnerability assessment approaches. Continuous monitoring and automated scanning are essential to adapt to the dynamic nature of cloud-based systems.

Shared Responsibility Model:

The shared responsibility model in cloud computing necessitates collaboration between cloud service providers and organizations.

Vulnerability assessments need to consider both the security measures implemented by providers and those managed by organizations.

4. DevSecOps:

Impact:

Shift Left Security:

DevSecOps integrates security practices into the software development lifecycle, promoting a "shift left" approach. Vulnerability assessments become an integral part of the development process, identifying and addressing issues early in the lifecycle.

Automation in Continuous Integration/Continuous Deployment (CI/CD):

Automation tools in CI/CD pipelines enable continuous testing for vulnerabilities. Automated scans run at each stage of development, providing rapid feedback and allowing developers to address issues promptly.

5. Threat Intelligence Integration:

Impact:

Contextual Insights:

Integration with threat intelligence platforms enhances vulnerability assessments with contextual insights. Assessors can prioritize vulnerabilities based on their relevance to known threats, improving decision-making in remediation efforts.

Real-Time Risk Assessment:

Threat intelligence feeds provide real-time information about emerging threats. Vulnerability assessments can leverage this information to assess the risk associated with vulnerabilities and respond promptly to changing threat landscapes.

6. Blockchain Technology:

Impact:

Decentralized Security:

Blockchain's decentralized nature introduces new security paradigms. Vulnerability assessments in blockchain environments focus on ensuring the integrity and security of smart contracts, consensus algorithms, and the overall distributed architecture.

Smart Contract Audits:

As smart contracts become integral to blockchain applications, vulnerability assessments include audits of these self-executing contracts. Assessors ensure that smart contracts function securely and as intended.

The impact of emerging technologies on vulnerability assessment is profound, necessitating a dynamic and adaptive approach to cybersecurity practices. Organizations must embrace these advancements, integrating AI, IoT considerations, cloud-specific assessments, DevSecOps methodologies, threat intelligence, and blockchain security into their vulnerability management strategies. As the technological landscape continues to evolve, staying informed and proactively addressing emerging challenges will be essential for maintaining robust cybersecurity postures.

13.2 Evolving Threats and OpenVAS's Role in Mitigation

In the face of evolving cyber threats, organizations need robust tools and strategies to identify and mitigate vulnerabilities. OpenVAS (Open Vulnerability Assessment System) plays a crucial role in this landscape, adapting to emerging threats and providing effective vulnerability management. This section explores the evolving threat landscape and outlines how OpenVAS can be leveraged to mitigate these threats.

Evolving Threat Landscape:

1. Advanced Persistent Threats (APTs):

Challenge:

APTs are sophisticated, long-term cyberattacks that aim to compromise systems and remain undetected for extended periods.

OpenVAS's Role:

OpenVAS assists in identifying vulnerabilities exploited by APTs. Regular scans and continuous monitoring enable organizations to detect and remediate vulnerabilities before they can be exploited by persistent threats.

2. Ransomware Attacks:

Challenge:

Ransomware continues to evolve, targeting critical systems and demanding ransom payments for data decryption.

OpenVAS's Role:

By conducting comprehensive vulnerability assessments, OpenVAS helps organizations identify weaknesses that could be exploited by ransomware. Timely remediation of vulnerabilities reduces the risk of successful ransomware attacks.

3. Zero-Day Exploits:

Challenge:

Zero-day exploits target vulnerabilities unknown to the software vendor, making them challenging to defend against.

OpenVAS's Role:

While OpenVAS primarily focuses on known vulnerabilities, its continuous scanning and integration with threat intelligence can aid in identifying potential zero-day vulnerabilities by detecting anomalous behaviors or indicators of compromise.

4. Supply Chain Attacks:

Challenge:

Supply chain attacks involve compromising software or hardware components within the supply chain to infiltrate target organizations.

OpenVAS's Role:

OpenVAS assesses the security of software components, identifying vulnerabilities that could be exploited in supply chain attacks. Regular assessments help organizations maintain visibility into potential risks.

5. Credential-based Attacks:

Challenge:

Credential-based attacks, such as phishing and credential stuffing, target user credentials for unauthorized access.

OpenVAS's Role:

OpenVAS scans can identify vulnerabilities related to weak or compromised credentials, guiding organizations in enforcing strong authentication practices and mitigating the risk of unauthorized access.

OpenVAS's Role in Mitigation:

1. Regular Vulnerability Scanning:

OpenVAS's primary function is to conduct regular vulnerability scans. By continuously scanning the network and systems, organizations can identify and remediate vulnerabilities promptly, reducing the window of exposure to potential threats.

2. Integration with Patch Management:

OpenVAS integrates seamlessly with patch management processes. It identifies vulnerabilities and aligns with patching strategies, ensuring that patches are applied promptly to address known security issues.

3. Continuous Monitoring:

Continuous monitoring using OpenVAS ensures that organizations stay proactive in identifying new vulnerabilities and adapting to emerging threats. Real-time assessments contribute to a dynamic and responsive security posture.

4. Threat Intelligence Integration:

OpenVAS can be integrated with threat intelligence feeds, enhancing vulnerability assessments with contextual information about emerging threats. This integration enables organizations to prioritize and respond to vulnerabilities based on real-time threat data.

5. Automated Remediation Workflows:

OpenVAS supports the integration of automated remediation workflows. This automation streamlines the process of addressing identified vulnerabilities, reducing manual efforts and accelerating the mitigation timeline.

6. Collaboration with Incident Response:

OpenVAS collaborates with incident response workflows. When critical vulnerabilities are identified, OpenVAS triggers incident response mechanisms, ensuring a coordinated and swift response to potential security incidents.

As the threat landscape evolves, OpenVAS remains a crucial tool for organizations seeking effective vulnerability management. By conducting regular scans, integrating with patch management, and adapting to emerging threats through continuous monitoring and threat intelligence, OpenVAS contributes to a proactive and resilient cybersecurity posture. Its role in automated remediation and collaboration with incident response further strengthens its effectiveness in mitigating evolving cyber threats.

As we conclude our journey through the realms of OpenVAS and cybersecurity vulnerability assessment, it is my sincere hope that this guide has served as a valuable companion in your quest for mastery. "**Mastering OpenVAS**" was crafted with the intention of not only imparting technical knowledge but also fostering a mindset of vigilance and proactive defense.

In your hands, you now hold a comprehensive resource that spans the spectrum of OpenVAS, from its historical roots to advanced customization techniques. You've navigated through the intricacies of vulnerability scanning, learned to interpret complex scan reports, and discovered the power of automation in assessments.

Remember, mastery is not an end but a continuous journey. As technology evolves and threats morph into new shapes, your commitment to staying ahead of the curve will be your greatest asset. Embrace the lessons learned within these pages and let them guide you in safeguarding digital landscapes.

May this book serve as a catalyst for innovation, a shield against emerging threats, and a source of inspiration as you continue to fortify the digital world. As you embark on your future endeavors in the cybersecurity domain, may you approach each challenge with the wisdom and confidence of a true OpenVAS master.

Thank you for joining me on this expedition into the heart of cybersecurity. Your dedication to mastering OpenVAS contributes to a safer, more resilient digital ecosystem.

Safe journeys, and may your path be forever illuminated by the light of knowledge and vigilance.

Made in the USA
Columbia, SC
28 August 2024

e594bb56-6b6f-4f72-8aea-a717b7a5889bR01